Roxanne

THE
UNICORN
BABY

Debunking 10 Myths
of Modern Parenting

Jonathan Ball Publishers

Johannesburg • Cape Town • London

Originally published in South Africa in 2021 by
JONATHAN BALL PUBLISHERS
A division of Media24 (Pty) Ltd
PO Box 33977, Jeppestown, 2043

This edition published in 2021 by
JONATHAN BALL PUBLISHERS
An imprint of Icon Books Ltd,
Omnibus Business Centre, 39-41 North Road,
London N7 9DP
Email: info@iconbooks.com

For details of all international distributors,
visit iconbooks.com/trade

ISBN 978-1-77619-143-7
eBook ISBN 978-1-77619-077-5

*Every effort has been made to trace the copyright holders and to
obtain their permission for the use of copyright material. The publishers apologise
for any errors or omissions and would be grateful to be notified of any corrections
that should be incorporated in future editions of this book.*
Cover illustrations by Lester Atkinson

Printed and bound in Great Britain
by Clays Ltd, Elcograf S.p.A.

For Zach
and Sophie

Contents

Introduction

I was anything but the perfect baby. I had terrible colic and big lungs, and managed to catch several illnesses in my first 18 months. I had so many courses of antibiotics in my first year that my front teeth rotted and had to be extracted by a dentist. Oh, and I was born with my one leg backwards so I required serial casting and a heap of physiotherapy. My poor parents, right?

My mother has always said that if I were her firstborn, she would not have had any more children. My mother also professes that my older sister was far easier than me and I must say the photographic evidence agrees. Every snapshot of my sister is filled with bouncy curls and big smiles.

However, despite my beastly beginnings, I went on to be a great kid. I mean, I even won the school prize for Love, Caring and Understanding in Grade three! I had a passion for helping others and it didn't take me very long to find the career of occupational therapy. In fact, I was 12 years old when I made up my mind.

A little premature, perhaps, for such a big decision but it made all my life choices surprisingly straightforward.

I loved university, cruised through community service and landed up working, as a graduate, with kids at a school for children with special needs called Vista Nova School. For me it had always been about paediatrics, so I was thrilled to get paid to do what I loved.

I quickly transitioned from the Education department to the Health department and found myself at Red Cross War Memorial Children's Hospital in Cape Town. Like Vista Nova, Red Cross was a melting pot of cultures, languages and medical conditions. I thoroughly enjoyed writing up assessments, home programmes and policy. I worked mostly with babies in their first two years of life and I loved my interactions with both the neurology and neurosurgery teams that I served. My patients came from all over Africa and it was not unusual for me to attempt to speak four languages in a single work day: English, Afrikaans, isiXhosa and French. The patients were diverse: every class and every culture made their way through those doors.

Unfortunately, I couldn't see how having my own family would be possible if I continued working at a tertiary academic hospital with such vulnerable babies, some of whom passed away. I didn't think I would be able to lose a patient in the morning and go home that evening to parent my own babies. Expecting to start my own family, I accepted a transfer to a smaller secondary hospital closer to home.

Victoria Hospital had fewer wards and fewer babies who died. It is served by top-notch clinicians who are also incredible human beings. I had both my babies while working at Victoria Hospital. During my time there, I forged deep friendships with a group of physiotherapists who ended up doing pregnancy and parenting alongside me. There's nothing like the camaraderie of mothers pumping breast milk in the lunchroom!

I had been practising as an occupational therapist for five years before my daughter arrived and I had many strong opinions on parenting. Like me, my daughter was not one of those seemingly perfect babies; consequently, the experience of having her humbled me – a very important step for me in becoming both a better therapist and a better mother. She challenged much of what I thought I knew and thought I was good at.

After reading many baby books and receiving a lot of bad advice, I became passionate about evidence. We are taught to be evidence-based practitioners and I became an evidence-based parent, leaning heavily on older, wiser health professionals whom I now call 'the Silver Foxes'. Just because a book says 'do X', it doesn't mean you should. I started looking for the evidence behind the therapy techniques I used at work, as well as the parenting techniques I had been told to use at home.

When my daughter was 18 months old and we had all found our parenting groove, I fell pregnant with my son. With new, more realistic expectations, our family managed far better this time around.

I had found it fascinating working as a mother and occupational therapist at Victoria Hospital where, again, there was so much diversity. I loved the healthy debate and the clear impact that culture had on parenting practices. It was not an easy decision to leave my position at the hospital to focus more on my own babies while I slowly grew my own private practice.

Private practice brought with it a completely different client group and an unexpected difficulty. The families I saw were mostly professionals who had been to university and were succeeding in their careers. They were intelligent, resourceful people who could find any information or product their baby or child needed. But some of them were suffering emotionally and were generally not thriving in their role as parents.

These parents had bought the book, downloaded the app and had the sleep expert in their home. They seemed completely hung up on what I have come to identify over the years as certain **myths of parenthood**. They were trying desperately hard to get it right but they were burning out.

South Africa is known as a world within a country because it is such a diverse place. In my clinical practice, I witnessed that the more Western the parenting expectations, the higher the level of parental anxiety. Some parents found it hard to not be in control and struggled with the fact that they couldn't change the way their baby was napping or feeding or refusing to go in the potty.

I often found that these parents had to rely on friends for support and did not have a larger community or family network to rely on. At times, those who came alongside them seemed to be more competitive than supportive. There was a strong focus on independence and mastery, rather than interdependence and learning.

At the hospital I would hear the Silver Foxes say, 'Give your baby time to . . .' but when I repeated the advice in my private work I would hear, 'I don't have time for this . . .'

It was during this season, raising two babies and building a business, that I had a conversation with my big sister who was seriously considering the prospect of raising her first child as an only child. She was still dutifully trying to get her baby, who was slightly younger than mine, to 'sleep through the night' and couldn't imagine having another child.

Her first pregnancy had not resulted in her dream natural birth. Breastfeeding had not gone according to plan and her baby had needed surgery to correct some pretty impressive ocular challenges. As a toddler, her daughter was an absolute delight but had chosen to walk to the beat of her own drum, especially when it came to sleep.

I kept my sister's hope for a second child alive by promising her that her next baby could surely only be easier than her first. She deserved to birth the elusive, perfect infant, or Unicorn Baby as I will refer to it in this book. After all, she had put in some serious extra shifts raising her first, hadn't she?

My sister did, in fact, go on to birth such a creature. But thankfully, for our relationship and all moms in her circle, she fully recognised that it had nothing to do with her parenting skills and everything to do with her son's biology. He was simply born a Unicorn Baby.

We laughed as he would drink the textbook volume, burp himself and fall asleep on his back in his cot in only a few minutes. We cried real tears when he slept through the night and woke to smile happily in the morning. He was sleeping through the night long before his big sister ever had.

He started losing some of his shine when he decided he would wait rather a long time to crawl and then, when he did get moving, he showed very little interest in walking. He was not following what the book said any more.

As my sister started re-exploring the realm of 'otherness' with her second child and his gross motor development, this book, my third 'child', was being birthed.

As a practising occupational therapist it was clear to me that when it came to parenting there was no easy road. No baby is a

Unicorn Baby in every respect. And very few Unicorn Babies grow up to be Unicorn Toddlers.

Every parent hits a bump somewhere in the first year. For some this happens early on, perhaps even while they are on their journey to becoming parents. You may not have planned to become a parent at all or your plans to conceive may have not worked out as your ovulation tracker said they would. If you have fostered or adopted, then your call to say 'your baby is ready for you' may have taken far longer or far shorter than you had thought it would.

Even if your beginning is a breeze, the bumps could come later – perhaps in the birth plan or birth story or perhaps in your (non-) breastfeeding story.

This book is for parents who want to know more about the mysterious being that is their baby. It is for the pregnant mom who is unsure of what she needs to do once her baby arrives and for the ambitious father who wants to give his child the best life possible. *The Unicorn Baby* is for moms and dads who feel they are not winning at parenting, who fear they may be messing things up. If you have ever asked yourself, 'Is parenting really supposed to be this hard?', this book is for you.

It is also for the new mom who might find herself feeling unexpectedly lonely on maternity leave, and for seasoned grand-parents who are interested to see what science says about what they have known all along. The book also addresses the concerns of the worried well – those who have gorgeous, healthy babies but can't seem to stop worrying: **'Is my baby going to be okay? Is this normal?'** It is for the parent who is used to succeeding and is looking for help to become a better parent.

I will be using my experience as an occupational therapist to debunk what I believe are the top ten myths of modern parenting.

Many parents get so caught up in these myths that it severely hinders their ability to care for their baby. Parents who believe there is a perfect plan to raise a perfect baby experience far more anxiety and far less satisfaction.

As you work through each of the myths discussed in this book, please remember that my heart is for babies and their parents, whomever they may be. Where you see 'parent' or 'mother', please know that I am talking about anyone who cares for and loves a baby. You may find this book helpful as a father, nanny, grandparent, aunt, or uncle, and my intention is not to exclude you.

I have included real stories from my journey as a parent, as well as from my clinical work. Names and a few details have been changed to maintain confidentiality. I am so grateful to the many babies, children and families who have taught me so much. I feel honoured to have been given the opportunity to walk alongside them when things were not okay.

Whether this is your first baby or your ninth, I hope you find *The Unicorn Baby* both entertaining and informative. You may be straight or gay, single or committed, have permanent or temporary parenting status at Home Affairs, or have come into parenting willingly or reluctantly. Whatever your credentials, this book is written for you.

What is a Unicorn Baby?

If you have read a few baby books or searched the Internet for parenting tips, you have most likely stumbled across the mythical Unicorn Baby. This baby is said to pee pure gold and poop rainbows. While most parents have heard about the Unicorn Baby, few have ever seen one.

The Unicorn Baby is elusive, so it may be easier to spot the parents of the Unicorn Baby. These parents will be looking good and claiming to feel great. This is largely because the Unicorn Baby has not changed their lives. Their Unicorn Baby has fitted seamlessly into the ideal routine as prescribed by an accredited, opinionated person. Their babies have breastfed with ease every four hours and, of course, slept through the night since they were six weeks old. Their Unicorn Baby grows and develops above the 50th percentile, leaving very little for their parents to work on or worry about.

These parents attribute their baby's success to their superior parenting practices, as well as the stimulation classes that are sure to turn their Unicorn Baby into an even more super baby. This will be the baby who not only hits their developmental milestones on time, but smashes them out of the park. They will go on to speak four languages thanks to a fabulous foreign language app.

Whether this baby exists or not does not really matter. What does matter is this: apparently, you did not get this baby. And that is probably why you are reading this book.

I believe the Unicorn Baby has risen to fame through a relatively new parenting phenomenon – online comparison. This generation of parents is the first to use both parenting books and online parenting advice that is available 24/7 via the Internet. Today's parents can gather data anywhere at any time about babies who are exactly the same age in weeks as their own baby. The Unicorn Baby has become the gold standard to which every other baby is compared, resulting in babies who are labelled as good or difficult based on unrealistic and at times even harmful expectations.

Parents seem to start with high expectations of themselves and then transfer these to their babies. With an insatiable appetite for (mis)information, parents can find themselves with a long list of dos and an even longer list of don'ts.

The lie is that you, too, can create your very own Unicorn Baby if only you follow certain parenting tips. Online articles and parenting books will describe a few easy steps that promise amazing short-term results, such as:

1. Your baby will sleep through the night.
2. Your baby will feed only every four hours.
3. Your baby will be able to fall asleep without you.
4. Your baby will play by themselves peacefully.
5. Your baby will learn to self-soothe.

You will be tempted to buy into these programmes because every parent wants their baby to feed less often, sleep more and fit in with their life. While this may or may not make parenting easier in the short term, it will definitely make parenting your baby more difficult in the long term. The reality is that there is no such thing as the perfect baby – and, equally, there is no such thing as the perfect parent or the perfect family or the perfect routine.

The many myths of modern parenting depend on the following central lie: if your baby does not comply with modern parenting norms, then there is something wrong – either with your baby or with your parenting. This is based on the assumption that all babies are born the same. They are all born a blank slate, void of any preference or personality, and so it is your job as the parent to programme them and make them comply. If the baby is not complying then it means that the parents have done something wrong and the baby has not been programmed correctly.

Perhaps the parents have not followed the right plan from the beginning? Perhaps they have been too undisciplined at implementing a good routine or have given in to their baby's cries, creating a baby who expects their needs to be met all day and night? The baby has a problem and must be 'fixed'.

Parents want as much success in their home life as they may have had in their work life. For them, the stakes are high and they do not want to get anything wrong. However, this only causes a heightened sense of fear and anxiety.

How does this generation of parents sort through the noise? Many find themselves parenting in isolation: living and working

16

far away from their families and the environments in which they themselves were raised. Many are juggling a career with raising a child or two, and simply don't have the time they need to wait for their baby to 'grow out of it'.

If you have often asked yourself the question, 'Is this normal?' with regards to your baby, then this book is for you. It offers parents a chance to understand their baby's biology and how it drives development. There is variation within the normal range, and this should be celebrated rather than feared.

How do you make your baby perfect for you? You don't. You choose to accept them for who they are just as they accept you for the parents you are. You get to know them – all of them – the good, the bad and the ugly. Just as they get to know all of you – the good, the bad and the ugly.

You get to know how they like to feed, fall asleep and be held. They get to know how you like to live, receive love and interact with them. Successful parenting is not about showing love only on special occasions (although these are pretty cool for any kid); it is showing children that they matter in many, very small moments over many years.

It is important to remember that no one is trying to be a 'bad parent' or to harm their baby. All parents want what is best for their children:

- We all want to belong to a family whose members love one another;
- We all hope for a family whose members stay in relationship with one another; and
- We all want a family that regards each member with fondness.

A biological and developmental road map

As a parent, you will quickly discover that each baby is different. They all have their own preferences and definite dislikes. Babies are not robots or simple organisms that require a few key ingredients to survive. They are real people with real needs – only, they come in much smaller packages . . . thankfully!

My hope is for you to see that, in some cases, your baby does not have a *problem* at all but that you, as a new parent, may have been misinformed by popular culture about what is normal at a given age.

If you get a glimpse of this book before hearing the myths of parenthood, then you are one of the lucky ones. If you are already bobbing about in a sea of guilt, riding waves of self-doubt, then the good news is that you are not alone. While you may feel out at sea with your one-of-a-kind baby, most of your friends and family members did not parent a Unicorn Baby either. Most likely, they also suffered through sleep deprivation, cried over spilt milk and tried every 'here comes the choo-choo train' feeding trick.

In the midst of their suffering, three things may have happened:

1. They found something that worked for them and their baby that made them feel successful and now they believe this way will work for every baby. Aloe juice, anyone?

2. Their baby got older and it got easier, which made them feel more competent, and now they will tell you it actually *was* easy and they loved every second of it (they didn't, but they are dedicated to the story that they were competent parents and had a good baby).

3. It was *so* bad back then that they have blocked it all out and now only remember the golden years starting with their child's first day of big school! They will tell you they don't remember anything about those first blurry years and can't give you any advice and this is actually their truth. Who knows, perhaps they needed to forget to stay committed to parenting their kid?

I decided to write this book before my own parenting glasses become too rose-tinted and while my clinical practice is still full of atypical babies that drive home the message again and again that Unicorn Babies are hard to find and that there are many variations of what is 'normal'.

My aim is to help all new parents discover that their baby is fearfully and wonderfully made. Yes, you should have equal parts of fear and wonder as you parent this ever-changing, ever-growing little being. I want to give you a biological and developmental road map of your baby that will hopefully help to point you in the right direction.

Most of all, you should understand how the hard work that you put in now (down in the trenches) becomes the firm foundation that is your relationship with your child as they grow older. So often, it is the parents of babies who had the rockiest start who end up with the strongest lifelong connections. Yes, I am still trying to find the meaning of my initial suffering as a mother!

Each of us has a physical network of thoughts and memories that has become our road map to life. We have conscious and unconscious ideas of what good parenting encompasses. These ideas will be governed by what we experienced as kids being parented and also what we have seen as adults regarding how other people have parented their kids.

Of course, once you actually become a parent you are adding to this with each new experience of parenting your baby. This pre-parenthood road map is helpful, but because our babies are growing and learning, our road map constantly needs to be reviewed and updated. For example, choosing to raise your kids just like your parents did is great, but it may not help you all that much when it comes to some of the new parenting challenges – like what to do with your cord blood, or how much screen time your baby should get, or whether you should follow the advice of a best-selling breastfeeding app.

If you hold your parenting opinions very loosely, this will be an easy, intriguing read. If you hold your parenting opinions tightly ('my baby will sleep in their own bed from day one') then you may want to pay more attention to the biology bits that underpin this book to understand why your brain may not have made the best parenting proclamations back in the days 'before children' (BC).

I give you permission right now to relinquish any well-meaning, but ridiculously naive, proclamations you made before meeting *your* baby. It's okay to change your mind and adjust your approach as you go along. I promise.

Why biology matters

When I say you need to consider your baby's biology, I am referring to the cells of your baby's brain and body. These cells are constantly growing and changing to allow your baby to develop. So, when I say a baby has a biological need, you should try to imagine this on a cellular level. A baby's biology creates a drive towards meeting that need, whether it is for energy, love, warmth, or play.

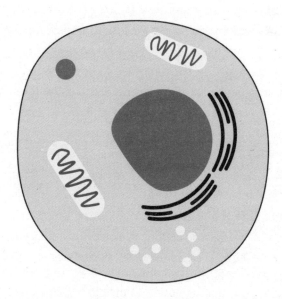

Cellular growth will support a developmental stage. What does this mean? Well, an easy example would be your baby transitioning on to solids.

To move on to solids, your baby will need to recognise the difference between food and non-food items. That recognition will happen thanks to growth in their memory centre after many, many hours of smelling, touching and mouthing both food and non-food items.

They may also need to bite down using their front teeth to select a manageable piece. That will be after growing front teeth after many, many hours of teething.

Once the food is in their mouth, they will be able to munch and swallow the food without gagging or choking after developing coordination of the lips, tongue and jaw. That will be thanks to many, many failed attempts where the food did not get swallowed but landed up on the floor.

This exposure, exploration and failure is what we call learning. Without these three ingredients, skills will not develop 'normally'.

Here is another example. A full-term baby is born 'knowing' how to suck. If left on their mother's chest they will crawl up and latch onto the breast. This process is driven by the sub-plate – a temporary structure in the brain that helps a baby do things reflexively or automatically. However, after two or so months this structure dies off and feeding becomes a more active process. A baby will have had exposure to the breast and learnt how to feed comfortably. They may have found a preferred position or a favourite side. Failure will have taught them to alter their approach to feeding, and so they may have a strategy in terms of feeding more slowly or for shorter periods or by using their tongue more than their jaw.

Development is a dance between biology and experience. Some babies will require more experience to learn than others. The golden rule is to respectfully introduce your baby to a wider variety of sensorimotor experiences, watching and waiting as their development unfolds.

Almost all babies will have an area of development that is tricky for them, be it sleep, feeding, talking, or teething. Oh, except for the Unicorn Baby, of course. The Unicorn Baby develops without exposure. The Unicorn Baby never fails. In fact, the Unicorn Baby does not rely on biology!

With that in mind, it is time to explore some of the myths of modern parenthood. Each myth can be read independently, so if you are more interested in one area than another, go ahead and jump around.

My hope is that, as you unpack each myth and replace it with its corresponding biological and developmental realities, you will feel more prepared. You will gain insight into and appreciation for your baby and your role as a parent. You will celebrate your baby's uniqueness, whether they have been born a Unicorn or not.

There has never been, and never will be, another baby just like yours.

Myth 1
Babies are all the same

The Unicorn Baby is born on their due date via easy natural birth and latches immediately. Their Apgar scores are a perfect 10. They have great genes, well-developed muscle tone and, of course, are the perfect size. Within their first year of life they learn to walk, talk and eat solids without a fuss. They have great personalities and easy temperaments. The Unicorn Baby favours what their family favours and dislikes what their family dislikes. They will grow up to be supremely intelligent, successful and well-rounded individuals.

All newborns are the same and need the same things, right? They have but a few basic needs that almost anyone can meet. They need milk, a nappy change and some warmth. It's really not very complicated.

Back in the day, these were the thoughts and attitudes of many so-called baby experts. It was thought that life started at the same point for all human beings – birth. Before that, there was nothing. A newborn was not thought capable of love or preference, or even of experiencing pain. It has only been in the past 30 or so years that the medical community has recognised babies as capable of experiencing and communicating both physical and emotional needs.

This myth that babies are all the same is the foundation on which much bad advice is offered to parents. It's the reason many parents feel drawn to compare their baby to other babies who are very close in age.

Why are some babies walking, talking and potty trained at their first birthday party, and others aren't? Why are some parents sleeping through the night from when their baby is four weeks old, and others are still dragging themselves out of bed when their baby is two years old?

The brain governs the body and, ultimately, behaviour. Inside our brains are billions of brain cells. Under a microscope, these look like little starfish. As the immature brain experiences life, the starfish will start to hold hands and form complex pathways and intricate networks linking different areas of the brain together. A baby that has many, healthy starfish and can make many attempts at a task will develop well. A baby with fewer starfish or with less frequent chances to attempt a task will develop more slowly.

For example, a baby who sees their mom's smiling face and hears their mom's voice many times a day will be more likely to try smiling and go on to start babbling and cooing. This baby will form a pathway between their visual centre, emotional centre and language centre. They will find making eye contact, smiling and cooing all at the same time easier and easier, the more they get the chance to practise doing this. The phrases 'cells that fire together wire together' and 'practice makes permanent' are often used by health professionals to explain this phenomenon of interconnectivity and efficiency.

However, if the brain cells are fewer or less healthy, or the baby does not see a smiling mom, then this pathway will not develop typically and the baby will not be inclined to smile when spoken to as other babies would.

At the end of the first year of life, apoptosis happens. Any brain cell that has not proved useful is culled, resulting in a death of roughly half your baby's brain cells. This sounds horrific, but the process actually allows babies in the second year of life to process information more quickly and use the successful pathways they do retain more efficiently.

Apoptosis may be the largest death of brain cells at one time, but culling will continue to happen throughout our lives. Brain cells that we do not use regularly will be removed. This is where the principle of 'use it or lose it' comes from in neuroscience. On the other hand, there is hope: brain cells will continue to grow as we learn new skills. The brain is described as plastic as it is constantly adapting. We are truly designed to be lifelong learners.

There are many factors that help or hinder these brain cells in forming and creating pathways. Factors that can impact how your baby responds to the world around them include genetics and culture, gestational age, birth weight, body size and proportion, muscle tone, medical needs and temperament or personality.

Genetics and culture:
Can you blame it on the genes?

A baby acquires so much from its genetic heritage or nature. Sex, height, intelligence, eye colour, handedness, skin colour, even hairiness . . . it is all written right there in your baby's DNA.

One of the easiest ways to see the impact of genes on development is through looking at twin studies. Twin studies compare identical twins (who share exactly the same genetic code) with fraternal twins (who share only half the genetic code). While biological siblings also share half the same genetic code, they are raised at different points in time, and therefore in differing environments, which could impact their development. By studying twins rather than siblings, it is hoped that the impact of environmental factors is limited.

The largest ongoing twin study in the world is the Twins Early Development Study that has followed 20 000 pairs of twins in England and Wales born between 1994 and 1996. This study has created 300 journal articles; one of its most notable findings, according to Kathryn Ashbury and Robert Plomin's book *G is for Genes*, has been the discovery that genes play the largest role (60–70 per cent) in determining a child's academic performance, especially in the primary school years. This finding shows that young children who are struggling to learn need early support, and not just more time to catch up with their peers.

On the other side of the debate, are those who recognise that the way in which a baby is nurtured plays a crucial role. These researchers recognise the influence of the environment. This includes culture, parenting and physical resources. The Millennium Cohort Study of 2000/2001 compared the attainment of developmental milestones in different demographics. Over the past 20 years, 18 827 children from diverse backgrounds have been studied at various ages, namely at 9 months, 3.5 years, 7 years and 11 years. This has produced over 700 journal articles that detail measures such as child development, cognitive ability and educational attainment.

It is well-recognised that certain countries seem to produce certain strengths. For example, Kenya is known to produce great runners; interestingly, a journal article by Charles Super indicates that in Kenya babies walk earlier than babies from other cultures do. Likewise, Japan is renowned for producing many great mathematicians. Japanese children can be relied on to score higher results in mathematics than children from other countries. And in his book *Educational Achievement in Japan* Richard Lynn tells us that young Japanese children score higher in non-verbal IQ testing than children from other cultures do.

What is more difficult to establish is whether these differences are maintained when a baby develops outside of that culture. Would a Kenyan baby walk as early if raised by a Japanese family? And would a Japanese baby be as good at understanding shapes if raised in Kenya?

It is now widely accepted that both nature and nurture are important. Epigenetics is a relatively new field that looks at how genes are switched on and off by environmental triggers. So, having an array of genes that code for running or for mathematics may not be enough: your baby may need these to be switched on through experiences. For running, this could be through engaging in rough play or being carried on their mothers' backs or having plenty of coarse sand under their feet while learning to walk. For mathematics, this could be growing up in a number-rich household with parents who sing and chat about number concepts and give a baby many different shapes to touch and play with when they are very little.

In short, **babies are genetically different and this means they will develop differently**. What works for one baby may not work for another. It is not either genetics or culture that will cause your baby to be one way or another – it is an interplay between the two. A variety of parenting strategies are necessary, as we are not raising clones.

Gestational age:
How long did you bake that baby for?

A baby is supposed to stay inside their mother's womb for 40 weeks. But many babies are born long before this. Full-term babies benefit from their time inside. They have more fat to keep them warm and provide energy; they have larger brains and more mature nervous systems, which cope better with noise and light; they have mature lungs that can collect oxygen from air; and they are compressed into the fetal position (hands and legs tucked in), which gives them an advantage when it comes to moving against gravity.

Premature babies may not be born in a physiologically stable state: they may struggle to maintain their body temperature, hate light and noise, and find touch painful. They may be putting a lot of effort into breathing and be unable to move off the surface that they are lying on. Therefore, some babies who are born at 40 weeks may develop more quickly than babies born at 34 weeks simply because they are older and born more ready for the outside world.

Birth weight:
My, my! Now that is a big baby!

If two babies are both born at 38 weeks, one weighing in at 2 kg and the other weighing in at 4 kg, the one weighing 4 kg may develop faster. Bigger babies often have a biomechanical advantage in that they have less space in the womb than smaller babies do, which means that bigger babies may be born with joints that are 'stiffer'.

Consequently, if a bigger baby is placed on their back, their legs and arms may remain slightly bent and pulled towards their middle. Even though they are no longer in the womb and are now under the effect of gravity, their body remains shaped in the fetal position. These babies will need less active control to move their hands to their mouths or their hands to their feet.

They will find moving far easier than babies who are starting to move from an extended or outstretched position. This gives them an advantage when learning to move their body and conquer gravity.

Body proportion and size:
Bigger is not always better

Proportion is a difficult thing to judge in young babies as newborn babies should have a head-to-body ratio of 1:3. To give you an idea of how top-heavy that is, an adult's head is only one tenth of its body size. So, your baby will literally be growing into their head for many years to come.

However, some babies have larger-than-average heads. These kids will obviously have to work harder to gain head control and may prefer to sit 'well stacked', with their heavy heads sitting on top of their little bodies, rather than to move in and out of the sitting position.

Taller or longer babies may have a harder time learning to control their longer limbs. They may also be unfairly judged as being slow if they are taller than the other kids their age. A giant one-year-old will be expected to speak and control their temper, while a petite one-year-old will be perceived by others as 'just fine', even if they are not saying any words and are pushing other babies away.

Muscle tone:
Did you get a floppy fish?

Tone is a very confusing concept for parents. All newborns are floppy: they need your help to support their head and keep their limbs together. However, some newborns are far floppier than others. A baby who is very floppy and therefore more difficult to pick up and handle will be classified as having low muscle tone or being hypotonic.

Having low muscle tone does not always mean that your baby has underdeveloped muscles or that your baby is weak. You can have low muscle tone and go on to develop strong muscles.

Muscle tone comes from the brain, as well as from within the muscle's structure. There are several parts of the brain that look after muscle tone, namely the motor cortex, cerebellum, striatum, red nucleus and basal ganglia. When a baby is asleep, the muscle tone will feel lower; when the baby is awake and excited, the muscle tone should feel higher. A baby whose muscle tone feels lower even when they are awake will have to use more energy to get going and make active movements. This means a baby with low tone will find it more difficult to initiate or start a movement and have more difficulty maintaining a position (such as holding their head up in tummy time or sitting upright on the floor).

Repetitive activities like breastfeeding, chewing and talking will also be more tiring for low-toned babies, so a baby with low muscle tone may develop more slowly within certain developmental areas than a baby who has typical muscle tone and feels more 'put together'.

Medical needs:
You can't ignore the hashtags

If you were to dive into a hospital folder you would see descriptors like this one:

4-month-old baby girl presenting with #LBW #GORD #URTI

These hashtags represent key medical diagnoses pertinent to your baby. In this example:

LBW = low birth weight;
GORD = gastro-oesophageal reflux disorder; and
URTI = upper respiratory tract infection.

Each medical diagnosis will put strain on your baby at a cellular level. If a baby is hospitalised for an illness, there may be a regression (losing skills that were present before getting sick) or stagnation (very little development made during this time). This is understandable as the body prioritises getting better over reaching developmental milestones.

The more hashtags your baby has attached to their name, the slower their development may be. Common infant hashtags that your baby may experience are jaundice, constipation, gastroenteritis (diarrhoea with/without vomiting), anaemia, middle ear infections, torticollis (head turned to one side), and colds and flu.

If your baby has regressed while ill, these skills should return when your baby is better. If your baby is struggling with chronic illness, you will need to be patient and accept that your baby may need more time than others to develop the same skill due to the medical challenges they are facing.

Temperament or personality: Which is it?

A baby is a little person and not all people behave in the same way. Temperament describes a baby's style of adapting. Generally, three temperaments are ascribed to babies:

1. **Easy temperament:** Happy-go-lucky babies who seem pleased to be born. They eat their food warm or cold and cope well in and out of the arms of their parents.
2. **Slow to warm up temperament:** These babies are 'easy' at home but become quiet and withdrawn with new people and in new environments. After 15 minutes or so they usually warm up and go back to being their normal selves.

3. **Difficult temperament:** These babies have been called 'fussy babies' and 'high-need babies'. They may seem to be displeased when out of their parents' arms and are impossible if out of their routine. They often have specific likes and dislikes from how they want to be held to how warm their bottle should be.

Personality, on the other hand, describes a baby's attributes. Some babies are introverts and others extroverts. Some crave novelty while others hate it. Some babies appear to be curious and others happy to be on their own. It is difficult to say where temperament ends and personality begins.

Some will say that while easy babies are easier to care for and easier to please, their happy disposition can make it difficult to tempt them to move out of sitting or to say a word to ask for something. Difficult babies, on the other hand, are thought to be quicker to move to get to where they want to be independently. They are also said to be strong communicators, who quickly learn how to protest when they do not like things and to request what they do want. Their persistence can mean that they get more practice than their easy-going peers and reach some milestones faster.

The same could be said for introverts and extroverts. Some babies are social firecrackers and just want to engage with others. Naturally, these babies will learn how to make friends, share toys and snatch toys back again more quickly than their more reserved peers. If your baby loves novelty, then enjoy novel experiences together. And if your baby is a homebody who seems unhappy in crowds, then make peace with the fact that you need to spend more time at home than out and about.

In my work, I have found that it can be limiting to categorise babies into three or four personality or temperament types. If only human beings were that simple! There are so many reasons why a baby may be behaving in a particular way and having an 'easy answer' may actually hinder you from truly understanding your baby.

This is why I always request that babies get a full medical assessment before being classed as 'easy', 'difficult', or 'fussy'. If you have subscribed to a 'one size fits all' approach you may misinterpret your baby's needs because of what you have read about that category of baby.

While the scenarios described below are rare (so please do not panic), I have encountered them over the years:

- An 'easy' baby who sleeps anywhere and never cries turns out to be hearing impaired.
- The 'difficult' baby who only wants to sleep in mom's arms turns out to have chronic middle ear infections.
- The 'fussy' baby who is a poor feeder turns out to be struggling with a food allergy.

Babies usually have a good reason to prefer things a certain way. They may be battling with colic or reflux, chronic itchy eczema, or a bout of oral thrush. Yes, it could be some gas or a bowel movement that is causing your baby discomfort. If your baby fusses and cries even after you have met their basic needs, there may be something wrong now, or something brewing.

Let's look at how all these factors that influence development may interact to create three very different newborn pictures. These are the three most common clinical pictures I see at my practice. I hope it helps to show why there is not a single solution that fits all newborns.

1. The floppy, lazy pre-term baby.
2. The full-term baby who is super sleepy.
3. The overdue big, hungry and strong baby.

1. A pre-term baby is a baby born before 37 weeks and who usually weighs under 2 kg. One third of a baby's weight is their head, so the lighter your baby the less their brain mass and the more vulnerable their brain. This is why we as health professionals lose our heads when babies weigh less than 1 000 g. We know it is hugely risky to have such an underdeveloped nervous system out in a world full of potential pain and possible infection.

A baby's gestational age (GA) is how old it is since conception. So we would say a pre-term baby born at 30 weeks who has been in hospital for six weeks is actually GA 36 weeks, while a baby born at 39 weeks who is now six weeks old is GA 45 weeks. Gestational age makes a huge impact on brain development. So while it is normal for babies to be sleepy and easy until four weeks old (GA 44 weeks), this could be longer for your baby if they were born prematurely. You should take their GA into account and correct their age for their first year of life.

For example, if your baby is 4 months old and was born 6 weeks premature, you would say:

$$\text{Corrected age} = \text{chronological age} - \text{weeks premature}$$
$$= 4 \text{ months} - 6 \text{ weeks}$$
$$= 16 \text{ weeks} - 6 \text{ weeks}$$
$$= 10 \text{ weeks old (or 2.5 months old)}$$

You should expect your baby to be developing like a 2.5-month-old and not a 4-month-old.

2. A super sleepy full-term baby could be a baby born between 37 and 40 weeks who has not yet fully awoken. They could weigh anywhere between 2.5 kg and 4.5 kg. They may fall asleep during feeds and sleep for up to 20 hours per day!

Do not be dismayed if suddenly, at about GA 44 weeks old, your baby seems to wake up on the wrong side of the bed and become far less content with the care you have been providing. You have not broken them. They are just starting to find themselves and may have discovered how to communicate in a language you understand – crying!

Plus, thanks to their weight gain they will have the energy they need to look around and kick their limbs . . . but also to complain when they are hot, cold, thirsty, full, tired, or awake and wanting some deeper sensorimotor experiences, or a little love. This complaining is actually a positive sign that your baby is progressing in the area of expressive language. Responding to your baby's communication means they will make more noises more often, which eventually turn into words, sentences and – a little later – stories.

3. An overdue and big, hungry and strong baby can often be incorrectly labelled as a loud or difficult baby, as they are often born in the 'awake and able to communicate' phase. What 'overdue' is differs from country to country. However, 'overdue' is generally viewed as a pregnancy that lasts for longer than 40 weeks. So, a baby born at 42 weeks could come into the world weighing in at 4.5 kg and won't fit into newborn clothing. This baby's brain would weigh 1.5 kg – the same weight as that of a premature infant!

The downside of this is that often these babies skip the sweet, drowsy, 'drunk' newborn phase completely. Their parents may be required to feed them more frequently, as well as interact with them more during the day.

There is far more variation possible than presented in the above-mentioned three pictures of newborns. What should start becoming clear is that there is a range of 'normal' newborns – and therefore a range of developmentally appropriate behaviours that will go with each biological phase or developmental stage. You will have an easier parenting journey if you can adapt your parenting to meet your baby where they are in terms of their biological development, rather than where you think they should be.

Trying to get a sleepy premature infant who is still using their energy to grow brain cells to 'wake up and do tummy time' would be unfair and unhelpful. However, an overdue newborn who is born with fair head control may love spending time lying on their mother's chest feeding and looking into her face. Trying to get this baby to sleep for 20 hours a day would also be unfair and unhelpful. There is no problem with either newborn – it is just that each baby is in a different phase of brain development and therefore needs different handling to thrive.

You need to adjust your expectations depending on your baby's age, stage and personal circumstances. Many things will affect your baby's development. As you can see, most of them are beyond your control. At any point, babies are working towards multiple developmental goals using every body system to do so.

Development is not linear. There are often pauses and leaps. Development in one area can mean a temporary pause in the development of other areas. For some babies, teething will negatively affect feeding and sleep, and even language development. While the development of teeth is a step forward for chewing solids and making new sounds, it may mean that the other developmental areas slow down to accommodate the new pearly whites.

Equally, the baby who sits first may not be the baby who speaks first or the baby who gets the best marks in school. Try to focus on the things that your baby is learning, instead of comparing them to other babies who are the 'same age'. Your outlook should be one of 'my baby can . . .' rather than 'my baby still can't . . .'

Development is equal parts science and wonder; you can never know for sure how your baby is going to turn out.

Nathan's story

Nathan was born at 36 weeks after a tricky pregnancy. His mom, Kelly, had been hospitalised at 30 weeks due to the onset of labour while she was at work. The labour was halted by her gynaecologist using IV drugs but what became clear on the scan is that Nathan had stopped growing at about 29 weeks as his placenta had calcified. He was not getting enough blood flow to get the nutrients and the energy he needed to grow, although he was able to remain alive. This phenomenon is called intrauterine growth restriction, or IUGR.

Despite remaining *in utero* until 36 weeks (which is usually great for lung development), Nathan was born weighing 1 600 g with no suck, swallow or breath reflex as is typical for a 29-week-old. This reflex emerges in about the 35th or 36th week of pregnancy, and helps a baby to coordinate breathing, latching and swallowing after the birth. Because Nathan's brain had effectively stopped growing or developing at about 29 weeks, he functioned like a 29-week-old and needed to be on CPAP (a respiratory machine that reminds him to breathe) and an NG tube (a tube that goes from his nose to his tummy to feed him without his needing to swallow).

I saw Nathan when his chronological age was eight months but he was still wearing clothing for three- to six-month-olds. He could sit if placed in a hunched-over position with his legs spread straight to widen his base of support and his hands stuck on the floor to prop himself up. He had bright eyes and a beautiful smile, and clearly adored both his parents. He had not yet rolled and could not tolerate tummy time. His parents were concerned about his small size and inability to crawl.

Because Nathan was born at GA 36 weeks (four weeks premature), his corrected age was seven months old. His gross motor development scored below four months old. This indicated a gross motor delay, even after adjusting for his prematurity. He had not learnt to lift his head when lying on his tummy, and could not roll or push up into or out of sitting. He needed therapy to help him tolerate weight on the palms of his hands and soles of his feet.

In this case, what was more important than Nathan's age at birth were the circumstances surrounding his birth. His low birth weight, long stay in neonatal ICU (NICU), and need for CPAP and an NG tube indicated that he had more risks in terms of brain development and/or meeting developmental milestones than other boys born at 36 weeks.

During sessions, we focused on helping him find his body and move through space to conquer gravity from different starting positions. It was with great joy that Nathan learnt to crawl, pull to stand and walk over the next few months, thanks to us going back and filling in what he needed to learn to start moving on his own.

In the field of early childhood development, age is important – but it is not everything.

Emily's story

Some babies are lucky enough to keep baking long after their friends have been born. Emily was one such baby, who came into the world at a whopping 42 weeks and a plump 4.3 kg. She was robust and strong. She had a great latch and fed beautifully.

She felt so solid that at four months you could plop her down into sitting and she would just balance there, showing off her gummy smile. Emily was the first grandchild on both sides, so she was justifiably adored. This meant lots of one-on-one interactions that helped her learn lots about communication. She said her first words at six months and became more and more chatty with each day that passed.

At 11 months, Emily was a pro at both sitting and giving orders. What she couldn't do was go anywhere. Not forwards, not backwards, not anywhere. She struggled to cope in any position other than sitting, so she took no weight through her hands and arms or her feet and legs. If she wanted something, she had to use her charm and growing vocal tones to get it.

Babies are born with a unique set of genes

Emily's maturity and size was a great advantage to her development in the first four or so months. But despite her having so many other strengths, it started to become more and more difficult for her to move around as she grew bigger.

Emily had a very different start from Nathan, but she ended up with a similar problem. In therapy, she quickly learnt to use advantageous movement patterns to get around. Her mom did well to use her good understanding of language to motivate and praise her efforts.

She is still as charming and chatty as ever, but has learnt that getting around on your own and choosing what you want to play with is quite fun indeed.

REALITY 1: Every baby is unique

- The Unicorn Baby needs very little other than milk, a nappy change and warmth, because babies are all the same, aren't they? Alas, not! They are different from day one. There has never been another baby exactly the same as yours.
- Babies are born with a unique set of genes, which are switched on and off by different things in their environment. Remember, cells that fire together wire together. Your baby is forming new brain pathways every time they try out something new.
- There are so many factors that can affect how your baby responds to the world around them. A few of these are genetics, gestational age, birth weight, body size and proportion, muscle tone, medical needs and temperament or personality.
- Because a newborn baby is governed by their biology, they will find what works best for their body in their own time.

Signs that you are busting Myth 1

✔ You recognise that your baby is a unique and wonderful person – capable of experiencing all kinds of emotions, from hysterical joy (at Daddy's silly faces) to deep despair (at Liony falling out the pram).

✔ Through trial and error, you have figured out what your baby prefers and dislikes, and you have started to uncover some quirks that you just love about your baby. Who knew a baby could be so passionate about ducks?

✔ You are working hard to try not to compare your baby to everyone else's babies.

✔ Every now and again you are amazed at how your baby has learnt to do something just from watching you. How cute is it when they attempt to brush their own hair?

✔ There is no perfect baby, just as there is no perfect parent. You can recognise both the wins and the challenges your baby faces.

Myth 2
A baby does not have to change your life

The Unicorn Baby fits into their parents' lives seamlessly. At home, they are happy to be held and fed by any willing caregiver. When out at the shops, they smile gorgeously at all passers-by. The Unicorn Baby naps wherever they are at naptime and would never mess with their mama's schedule. The Unicorn Baby is predictable and adaptable, and does just what the baby books say they will. Their parents' lives can go on as they did before their baby entered the world, only with more glitter and rainbows.

If you are not raising a Unicorn Baby, then I am sure your world has been rocked wildly – albeit wonderfully – since your baby entered the world. If you are trying to find a new normal, then busting Myth 2, the myth that a baby does not have to change your life, is a good idea.

I remember it so clearly: the day my gorgeous friends with no kids (FWNKs) summoned me to coffee to swear with a raised hand that having a baby would not change my life. They were concerned that I would lose myself to this baby, like every other friend who had recently become a mom. They wanted me to promise that I would still make time for gym, get to book club and attend any weddings that popped up in the next few months.

I was advised to get back to my old life as quickly as possible so that the baby would get used to how things were. What I gleaned from this conversation was that winning at the mom gig comprised the following three steps (in no particular order):

1. Getting your body back;
2. Getting your career back on track; and
3. Getting your social/sexy groove back.

Six weeks seemed to be the magic number that was thrown around the table. 'Don't worry! You should be running again at six weeks'. 'Don't make your hubby wait too long, hey! Definitely not more than six weeks'. 'By six weeks your milk supply will be stable and you can start pumping and dumping!'

I had clear instructions to show this baby who was boss. 'The trick is to make your baby *part* of your life, not make your baby *your whole* life,' was the advice I heard. My FWNKs were not being mean or selfish. They did have my best interests at heart. They loved me, and what they had with me. But what none of us had considered was what my baby's best interests might be.

Motherhood: There's no going back

Enter the real deal: an actual baby that belongs to you. Yes, keeping this baby alive is on you – forever. And no one seems to be too fazed about that. I mean, they let you walk out of the hospital without even completing a questionnaire?

A few weeks into mothering, while you are still regularly checking that your sleeping baby is breathing, the questions come again: When are you going back to work? Do you think you will get back to your pre-baby weight? Is everything back to normal down there?

This word 'back' infuriates me. There is no going back here, folks. Back is gone. 'Getting back to normal' is a dirty lie. It is an empty promise that is going to rob you of the joy of having a baby.

Unless you discover the trick of turning the clock back, you are never getting back to normal. Ever. Having a baby is not an acquisition, it is actually a loss, a bereavement of your pre-baby self. This is a new life you have been given, which means your old life, it is dead. Yes, dead! You know, the life where you were in control and scheduled your sleep, your work, your play? You need to stop the CPR, sit back and see the cold, hard truth.

You're not getting your body back . . . you're making a new one

When many people consider the idea of postpartum recovery, they think about weight loss and pelvic floor exercises. Yes, postpartum is a time to recover from pregnancy and birth, but it is also a time to rebuild both your physical and mental health.

Dr Nils Bergman, a Cape Town-based neuroscientist, has shown over and over again how becoming a parent can cause advantageous, permanent and irreversible brain changes that make moms and dads more suited to their new roles and gives them the parenting abilities to ensure their newest family member's survival.

The hormones oxytocin and prolactin that support birthing, bonding and breastfeeding actually rewire the adult brain to interpret the most awful sound (a baby crying) as a sound that requires caring, rather than hostility. A baby's cry cues their parents to run towards them, while those who do not share a bond with the child will want to run away from them. The parents will secrete more bonding hormones, while others will secrete stress hormones and promptly leave the scene.

Skin-to-skin contact has been shown to assist these brain changes and reduce the stress response that occurs in the brain when exposed to the sound of crying. The good news is that it seems to be helpful at any stage of the parenting journey. So, whether you do it at the birth or during the first few months that follow, invest in some brain-altering cuddles and help set yourselves up as concerned carers rather than hostile strangers.

You're not getting your evenings back . . . you'll be parenting 24 hours a day

Babies are not born knowing the difference between day and night. It takes a few months for a baby's circadian rhythm to appear.

Young babies are fragile and vulnerable and require around-the-clock care. They need their parents for warmth, security and food. As babies grow, their needs change and they do start giving you more time to sleep.

However, once you have had a baby, you will never switch off completely again. You will sleep more lightly than before, your body ready to respond.

Your mind will keep going back to your baby, no matter how hard you try to keep it from doing so. When you're at work, at gym, at the shops, your mind will be balancing these realities: what you are doing right now, and what your baby is doing right now, and what needs to be done once you're back with them. This acute awareness is due to changes in your biology. Your brain has rewired so that you can become a parent. Your survival instincts now extend to your baby. Caring for your baby has changed you.

Are they safe? Are they happy? Are they napping? And did they get at least a little bit of greens in? Your new responsibility will be with you not from the day they are born, but from the day you first find out that you are pregnant.

Parenting should really be called sacrificing. Even from that first acknowledgement of your fetus's hormone levels, you will sacrifice caffeine, alcohol, smelly cheese, your sleep, your appetite, even your breathing space. You can fight it, but parenting is happening to you.

But the joy – oh, the joy! – that death of the old can bring. And when you do rush home and miss the office birthday drinks to be met by a butternut-sodden smooch, well, it's going to be worth it . . . most of the time.

From the ashes of your old life comes the beauty of this new one. Do yourself a favour and breathe that newness in. There's no going back but there's a whole lot of life going forward. It's okay to miss the way things were.

You're not getting back to the way things were as a couple . . . you're becoming a family

Many couples pursue the goal of 'getting back to how we were before we had a baby'. The trouble with this is that, as discussed above, you are no longer the same people. Your brains have been rewired and your responsibilities, routine and roles have needed to adapt too.

Having a baby is the birth of not one but three new people: baby, mother and father. It is also a death or loss of self and how things were, and it's okay to feel sad about it and talk about the things you miss when it was just the two of you.

You are both growing alongside your baby, and there is going to be a lot to work out. It's ironic because now that there are three of you there is suddenly a lot more to discuss, but a lot less time to do so. Strong teams emerge when required. There's nothing like running out of nappies in the middle of the night to help you forge even stronger bonds.

As your new family is forming, you may be astonished to fall in love, not only with your new baby, but also with a new side of your partner – the loving parent. Watching your partner care for you and love your baby is only going to increase those bonding hormones.

What is critical during this time is to give your new family the time and space it needs to form. Watch, wait and wonder together as you learn more about your baby. You will need to learn to roll with the punches and hold your expectations of the day a lot more loosely than you did before.

In the introduction, we looked at how inappropriate expectations or road maps can make parenting more difficult. This could be an area that trips you up. If you expect to have the same freedom in your career, as much time with your partner, as much money to dispose of and as much freedom to socialise after you have your baby, then you will find it harder to accept your new life as a parent.

You may have caught a glimpse or two of parents winning as they were out and about with their babies. This may have given you the false impression that life with a baby can go on as it did before, except with a few cute pieces of baby equipment.

Yes, you can take your baby out in a sling, let them sleep in their car seat while you have lunch together or sit in their pram while you run errands. Just like you can go to the moon in a space-ship with an oxygen mask. However, the truth is that the output, or what is required to get there, may just not be worth going there that often. Depending on your baby, of course.

You see, the planning and preparation and packing that is required to do things with a baby in tow is hugely energy-demanding and the entire outing can end up being unsuccessful for many, many reasons that are beyond your control.

Hear that again: *reasons that are beyond your control*. Babies change all the time. Some days, they may sleep more and eat less. Others, they may cry more and eat more and need you more. So, give yourself a break: don't take too much credit when it works out, and don't take too much blame when it doesn't.

I had great expectations of a maternity leave well spent, myself, nursing my first baby on the beach over the summer. 'What could be easier than cuddling under an umbrella all day with your newborn?' I thought.

So, no, you cannot stop your baby from changing your life. A baby with an immature brain cannot fit into an adult world. Young babies need far more attention and care than many people anticipate. Study after study shows that, the more parents put in, the more babies get out – and, actually, the more parents enjoy their new roles.

In raising a child, there is no skipping ahead to the good parts. Spend your time in the trenches first, building a strong foundation. Then, you can expect to be a part of a strong family. Yes, the ultimate goal is to have kids that can fit into the adult world. But this goal can only truly be achieved by the time their brain is mature, at about 25 years old. Feel free to gasp. Parenting is a long road.

Finding your new normal

While the birth of a baby is reason to celebrate, it often throws new parents into a period of crisis. This period of intense change is sometimes called postnatal adjustment. Having a baby could mean that you move homes, change career paths, buy a family car and find new friends. These are all great things, but they mean change – and even positive change can be stressful. As with any crisis, you need as much help as you can get until you find your new normal.

Finding your new normal requires you to be present with your baby and communicate with your partner. But how do you find time to be present when there is suddenly a baby who needs so many things from you, not to mention all the other non-baby-related responsibilities you still have to see to? Here's how to thrive, rather than just survive.

Give yourself time off work to get to know your baby

This means time away from both paid and unpaid work. Taking whatever maternity and/or paternity leave you are granted is the first step in giving your family the gift of time. The next step is letting go temporarily of all other unpaid work activities that you may have taken on.

What unpaid work is differs for each person. Some may view cooking as work – a duty that they must perform daily within their family. It is their role ('I am the cook') and it gives them a feeling of productivity ('I made supper'), but it does not give their life meaning or purpose. Others may view cooking as a leisure activity – a chosen hobby that brings them great joy. It leaves them with a feeling of relaxation. For some, cooking is arduous; for others, it is refreshing. Some won't miss cooking; others couldn't imagine living without being able to cook.

I am not saying stop everything you do. However, you would be wise to plan ways to pause, limit or outsource meaningless work tasks where possible.

- Accept help from family and friends. There is a reason why, in so many cultures, extended family plays a huge part in looking after the new family.

- Stock up on nutritious frozen meals that are easy to prepare.
- Think about using the laundromat or purchasing a dish-washer.
- Temporarily lower your standards when it comes to house-work.
- Call in a cleaning service or gardening service for the first two months.
- Shop for your groceries online.

Give yourself time away from social commitments

Another way to make some time and space for your new family to form is by pausing as many social commitments as you can.

- Clear your calendar for the first two months. Birthday parties, weddings and holidays may not be that much fun with a newborn baby around.
- Once your baby is born, you can always say 'yes' if you are in a good space, but clearing your calendar allows you to manage the expectations of others. If it is generally well-known that you are planning not to socialise, then no one takes it personally when you turn them down. You will find it refreshing how much easier it is to say 'no' now that you are a parent.
- Take a leave of absence from social media platforms. It may be your side hustle, but it will need to wait while you bond with your new baby.

I often get asked by pregnant moms: 'If I'm not working and I have people helping me, then what am I meant to be doing all day?' Your job during these early days is to get to know your baby. By watching your baby, you will start noticing when they are hungry, tired, sore, or bored. You will notice that they are growing – in size, weight and needs – and that they will want you around, both day and night. Without realising it, you are figuring out how your baby works and becoming the expert on your baby.

As you find your new normal, you may naturally start to take back roles and responsibilities that you had before having a baby. Some will be anticipated, and even have a start date (such as going back to your job), while others will return unnoticed and uncelebrated (such as starting to cook again). You may also quite naturally let go of some roles and responsibilities that no longer work for your family. There is no right way to make a family – thank goodness for that.

Give yourself permission to change your mind as many times as you need to, and feel free to let go of any plans that are not serving your family well. If it works, keep it; if it doesn't, dump it. The plans, not the baby!

My story: The early days

I remember wanting to take my first baby for a walk around the block. She was four weeks old; I had cabin fever. Easy peasy breezy, right? The idea was to take a walk from 09:30 to 10:00 each day. But the morning ended up looking like this:

08:45 Fed baby on left side 20 minutes, right side 5 minutes. *What if that was not long enough on the right? Did I do the wrong boob first again? What if baby needs more milk?*

09:10 Baby refuses to suck after kind offers of more, so start burping, using all three techniques as demonstrated by the chiropractor on YouTube.

09:30 No burp in sight and baby has fallen asleep. *Maybe baby is getting better at sucking and there is no burp? That would be great! Time to give up on the burp.*

09:45 After several attempts the sling is on, and looks mostly feasible. *But damn, this thing is hot. It's February! Need to remove more clothing. Is a feeding bra and sling appropriate for a walk around the block? Definitely not with this much loose abdominal skin flapping about. Need to find light, cotton top with buttons that will allow for fast breast access in case baby did not, indeed, drink enough from right side.*

10:00 Insert sleepy baby into sling. Step around bedroom door and head flops severely to right-hand side. *Will she break her neck or stop breathing or . . . wake up?*

10:01 She is awake and red-face angry at the idea of being squeezed into the sling I made. *I thought she loved me. Seems I may have been wrong.*

10:05 Vom-bomb down my cleavage. *Perhaps I shouldn't have tried to get her to drink more? Is this a posset or a vomit? Does this mean I fed her too much? Or need to feed her again? There's a series of terrible words going through my head.*

10:35 I have changed baby's clothes and my clothes. We are back in the sling and heading for the door. *Here I come, post-baby world. Are you ready to see the world, baby girl? Random thought: what if I get chased and can't run as fast as I used to? Why am I having these crazy thoughts about our safety? What has happened to my brain?*

10:37 She has made a gigantic orange poo and it is spilling out the sides of my six-metre-long sling wrap. *How much poo can such a small thing make in one go? I must retreat to the land of baby changing stations.*

11:20 There is a mountain of laundry. *It is now so damn hot that this walk idea will have to wait until at least 15:00 when it cools down. Not that we could go right now, anyway, as baby wants to feed. How did two hours go by so quickly?* A walk around the block feels as far away as my next full night's sleep.

Sure, this is the beginning. It does get easier with time. The feeds and poos and voms do get further apart, and the day sleeps do get longer and then shorter and then disappear entirely somewhere around the age of three. But the mom and dad you see out and about, enjoying a stroll with their newborn? They may have hit the baby-life jackpot today. That mom with a newborn on Instagram baking gluten-free brownies? She posted a highlight from a shitty week. Let her have her brownie-baking joy, okay? Don't compare your everyday parenting reality to other people's highlight reel.

My story: Work in progress

A close mom friend and fellow occupational therapist, Jesse, and I were out with our kids at a petting zoo. At this stage we both had two kids under three years old and were celebrating getting out the house and actually *seeing* each other.

She noticed an unfortunate-looking mother guinea pig, who was clearly having a rough time with four bois-terous babies chasing after her, desperate to drink and snuggle and play. She looked frazzled, des-perate not to be found; her babies looked absolutely healthy, cute and full of energy.

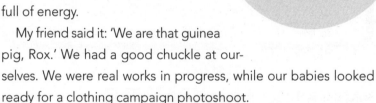

My friend said it: 'We are that guinea pig, Rox.' We had a good chuckle at our-selves. We were real works in progress, while our babies looked ready for a clothing campaign photoshoot.

There is a season that requires losing your old self to find your new self. It is messy. It breaks you before it rebuilds you. But you will emerge on the other side as a mother, a father, a parent.

USEFUL ACTIVITY

A wise nursing sister, Cindy Holmwood, advises all expectant parents to draw up a pie chart to represent each parent's typical before-kids day versus what they anticipate this will look like once their baby has arrived. Baby already here? No problem. This is still a useful learn-ing activity to do while you are furiously rethinking your roles and work schedules.

REALITY 2: Your baby will change your life

- The Unicorn Baby fits into their parents' lives seamlessly. Your baby may not. And that's okay.
- Focus on creating a new life with your new baby, rather than on trying to get back to your old life. Grieve the loss, and then celebrate your new normal. There is much joy to be found in this newness.
- Give yourself permission to let go of any plans that are not serving your family well. If it works, keep it, if it doesn't dump it. Parenting maps will need to be updated regularly. Don't hold on to any expectations too tightly.

Celebrate your new normal

- Watch, wait and wonder as you learn more about your baby.

Signs that you are busting Myth 2

✔ You have spent time doing skin-to-skin with your baby, either straight after the birth or when you both were strong enough to try it out.

✔ You have devised a new normal survival plan. You have given yourself time off work, both paid and unpaid, to get to know your baby.

✔ You have made some space for your new family to form by pausing as many commitments as you can. You have outsourced less important things (like cooking and cleaning) to friends and family for the first few weeks while you find your groove.

- ✔ Your baby is growing in size and weight, and needs and wants you both day and night.
- ✔ Your baby feels comfortable telling you when they are hungry, tired, sore or bored. It's tiring, but a good sign.
- ✔ You are growing – you are communicating what you need more to your partner and beginning to work as a team when there is a crisis, like running out of nappies.
- ✔ You are figuring out how your baby works and have become the expert on your baby.

Myth 3
You need to get your baby into the perfect routine

The Unicorn Baby is easily moulded. They do what their parents want them to do when they want them to do it. They stick to the chosen schedule. They follow the rules and they always play ball. If their parents want them to have longer stretches between feeds, they will do so. If they want them to nap for one hour or two hours, they oblige. They know that their parents are in charge and that it is their job to do what they need them to. It is in the Unicorn Baby's best interests, after all. They are easy-going and respond well to change.

Just as there is no such thing as the perfect baby, there is no such thing as the perfect routine. Despite this, you will find many published versions of exactly that: the perfect routine. So-called baby experts are quick to publish their versions with titles such as 'A newborn routine that works for every baby' and 'The perfect schedule for your baby'.

If you look a little deeper into the experts' credentials, they are often experts of their own genetically similar children. Translated, this means they have used one schedule successfully on their own babies. This is wonderful for them but it does not mean that this sacred schedule will work with a variety of babies or families. Remember, they have raised babies with different genetics from yours, in a different family, often living on a different continent from you and your baby. They are living in a completely different environment and are part of a completely different culture.

Yet, you will want to follow their routine, because it seems so, well, perfect. And because you are fearful:

- You have heard that babies do better when there is a routine.
- You believe that there are certain rules about feeds, awake time, or sleep that are better for your baby.
- You are worried that you will not know what to do if you don't have a recipe to follow.
- You want to know what's coming next: you need to be able to plan your life.
- You want to be a good parent and do the right thing.
- You are worried about getting it wrong. What if you create a bad habit that you won't be able to change ever again?

Ironically, I see many children at the practice who struggle with daily activities because of an early history of strict routines and excessive pressure from their parents. They battle with toileting, feeding aversions and bedtime anxieties. By trying to control your baby's future, you may end up disrupting it.

But you still want the perfect routine. I get it. Let's look at two examples of newborn routines: Schedule A and Schedule B. Have a look and compare them. Which one would you choose to implement?

Schedule A
A nap lasts for 1 hour and 50 minutes. A catnap lasts for 15–30 minutes.

8:00 Wake up and feed
8:40 Down for a nap
10:30 Feed on waking, then play
11:10 Down for a nap
13:00 Feed on waking, then play
13:40 Down for a nap
15:30 Feed on waking, then play
16:10 Down for a nap
18:00 Feed and bath
18:30 Down for a catnap
20:00 Put baby to bed for the night

Schedule B
This schedule assumes that your baby naps for 60 minutes and is awake for 90 minutes. Some babies' awake and nap times may be shorter or longer than this.

7:30 Awake
9:00 Nap
10:00 Awake
11:30 Nap
12:30 Awake
14:00 Nap
15:00 Awake

16:30 Nap
17:30 Awake
19:00 Nap
20:00 Awake
21:30 Bedtime

It should be really confusing to you that the two routines look so different. Which one do you follow? Let's compare them.

1. Schedule A is saying I get to sleep an extra 30 minutes in the morning, which seems great. It also says bedtime is at 20:00, which is a whole one and a half hours earlier than Schedule B. Schedule A means my baby and I get more night sleep.

2. Schedule A allows for five feeds a day, and Schedule B makes no mention of number of feeds. Assuming that, using Schedule B, you will feed with each waking, that is seven feeds per day. Schedule A seems like a little less work.

3. In Schedule A, the naps last for 1 hour 50 minutes. And there is one catnap of 15–30 minutes. That means that you get 7 hours 50 minutes of day sleep. Schedule B shows only 5 hours of day sleep, and it has a disclaimer stating that 'some babies' awake and nap times may be shorter or longer than this'. I don't like that uncertainty and I like that Schedule A means more day sleep.

Which schedule would you pick? Both promise to be great for your baby, so surely you should pick the one that seems to offer the most benefit to you as a parent? This is not a trick question.

You can pick whichever schedule you want to. In reality, though, you do not actually get to choose what your baby does, when. They do.

What should you do if your baby wakes in the middle of the night, or seems ready for the day before 07:30? Neither schedule runs through the night, so what are you supposed to do when your baby is awake in the dark hours? Is it assumed that these babies are sleeping through the night?

Many parents want to know what the perfect routine is because they know and believe that a routine is a good thing. So do I. It can be a good thing, but only if it is relevant and meets your baby's needs. A baby grows and changes every day, so you will need to hold your routine loosely. Think *fluid routine*, not *strict schedule*. Don't be surprised if your baby drops a feed today, only to start cluster feeding tomorrow. Or naps for two hours today, only to catnap tomorrow.

But if you don't have a plan to follow, how will you get it right? Together, you and your baby will figure out what works over time through watching, waiting and wondering. Oh, and yes – through failing. A lot of failing. For that is what teaches us the most.

Fail, fail and fail again

The brain is an interesting organ: it reorganises itself every day until we die. Failure, or the experience of something not working as we thought it would, can cause us to rethink – a process in which those little starfish we spoke about earlier may stop holding hands, realign to change position, or even die off completely. All because of failure.

Failure is the only reason that babies and parents change the way they are doing something. A small failure, like rolling too quickly and getting a fright, will mean that the next time your baby rolls they are more cautious and less likely to roll so quickly. The initial failure (and probably many more after that) will mean that, in the end, your baby can roll with control.

The same will go for your parenting. You will have certain instincts and certain theories. You will try them out – keeping the ones that work and looking for new ones where your best efforts fail. Perhaps, today, you will feed your baby too much and notice how uncomfortable they are. Tomorrow, you will change this as you have learnt what volume suits your baby. A few days later, you may notice that your baby is ravenous and that they suddenly need a greater volume. And so you will start to feed for longer or give bigger volumes.

Failure is learning, for you and your baby. Give yourself permission to get it wrong, because you will – many, many times.

Without the Unicorn Baby in your arms, what should your daily routine include? I know you want a predictable routine against which to measure yourself but I am not going to give you one. You know that all babies are unique and that they have fluctuating needs, so you are going to learn to read your baby and adjust your plans accordingly.

Rather than aiming to control your baby's feeding, sleeping and pooping (which is futile), focus on achieving these parenting goals of the first year: i) regular bonding, ii) building trust, and iii) sharing joy. If you can do these three things daily, you have found your perfect routine, whether your day or night goes according to schedule or not.

Whether your baby does five feeds or eight, takes three naps or four, is not what ensures a happy, healthy baby and family. Research keeps showing that a secure attachment is what determines long-term outcomes, not the routine you choose. How do you build a secure attachment? Let's look at three practices that help to establish and maintain this. Focus on achieving these things and you should have more good days than bad ones with your baby.

Regular bonding

While bonding begins during pregnancy, it intensifies for the whole family the moment they meet their newborn. The Sacred Hour is the first hour after a baby's birth. It is a time of uninterrupted skin-to-skin contact between mother and baby, and usually ends after a baby has had their first breastfeed. The Sacred Hour is a very precious time when a family forms, and is part of postnatal care in most hospitals. It needs to be protected as far as possible. If there is a medical reason that delays immediate skin-to-skin contact with your newborn, the Sacred Hour will begin as soon as possible after assessment from the care team. There is evidence that newborns placed skin to skin experience less stress and parents show more confidence in caring for their newborn. Yes, skin-to-skin can be done on fathers too.

Another practice that ensures bonding is baby wearing or baby carrying in the fourth trimester. The fourth trimester is the first 12 weeks after a baby is born. This can promote overall baby and parent health and wellness. For your baby, this ongoing skin-to-skin closeness assists with safety and warmth as well as access to regular feeding. It also provides them with skin-to-gut immunity through microbes ingested from the parents' skin, and can even diminish your baby's subjective experience of pain.

For parents, skin-to-skin has many benefits too: it can help reduce postnatal anxiety, increase a mother's milk supply, aid deeper and longer sleep times, and reduce the perception of pain post delivery.

There is a long-term change that occurs during skin-to-skin contact. There is a rewiring of both the baby and the parents' brains.

Yep, this closeness causes a structural change in your brain, as well as in your partner's and your baby's. Forever. Thanks to a rise in the love hormones prolactin and oxytocin, both the baby and those involved in bonding will experience a profound and clever brain restructuring. Neurons detach and reconnect to allow a baby and their mother and father to enjoy a magical synchronisation.

For example, as the baby's temperature drops, the mother's brain detects this and so increases the temperature of the skin on her chest. As the baby starts to become hungry and cry, this sound causes the mother's brain to signal letdown of breastmilk to feed the baby. When the baby fusses, the mother's body responds with more love hormones that assure that the baby receives care and understanding rather than rejection and frustration.

Fathers may not be able to produce milk or vary the temperature of their chests, but they can still benefit. New mothers and fathers who do skin-to-skin experience fewer stress hormones (such as cortisol and adrenaline) in response to their baby's crying than those who do not.

Babies do not know that they are separate from their mothers. They are therefore 'bonded' to their mother before birth. However, for mothers and fathers, bonding is often a more cognitive decision ('I am going to try bond with my baby now') before it is a natural, emotional connection ('I am so in love with my baby'). Give yourself time to get to know your baby and do not feel guilty if your new bundle feels like a stranger. In many ways, they are.

This 'oneness' or synchronisation is essential to the baby's survival and the mother's perception of her capability as a mother. A strong bond can boost a baby's and mother's mental wellbeing for years to come. A strong bond with a father ensures co-parenting in the early days and offers a baby the chance to learn many new things through a different kind of bonding and interaction.

It is only once a baby starts to become mobile and move away from their parents that they suddenly realise that they can be separate from their mother – a terrifying idea, as mother is a source of all good things and key to survival. However, equally enticing is the big world away from mama that offers new things to explore, taste and touch – the world that appears to belong to their father.

And so a healthy attachment allows a baby to slowly sway back and forth between dependence and independence on their parents with a secure, strong bond that is never doubted, whether the baby is near or far from them. 'Mom and Dad will help me if I need them. They will come back. They will come to me if I call out to them. They are there if I need them. I've got this.'

A securely attached baby will laugh or cry when they see their mother after a separation. Be concerned if your baby ignores you or rejects you when you return – it may mean that they have been separated for too long and experienced unhealthy stress. This can happen if you leave your baby regularly for extended periods. For example, it could happen if you are hospitalised, fail to see your baby when they are awake for a few days in a row, or go away on a holiday with your partner and leave your baby with someone who they do not care for.

If they are unsure of their secure attachment, they will be unsure whether they should re-attach again once you return. If this does happen, you should be intentional about reconnecting and reassuring them that when you go you will come back as promised. This brings us to the second goal: building trust.

Building trust

Secure attachment breeds secure children who grow into secure adults. Having their basic needs (warmth, food, protection) and their emotional needs (security, attention and trust) met by an attentive parent gives a baby an understanding of the world around them: 'My needs are legitimate, my family listens to me and the world is a safe, nurturing place to be explored and discovered. If it all gets too much, there is a place I can retreat to, where I will be supported and forgiven and loved no matter how badly I have failed.'

Not having their basic and/or emotional needs met consistently by a responsive parent gives a baby an understanding of the world as follows: 'What I need is not important. My family does not listen to me and the world is a cold and harsh place that is to be approached with caution and fear.' This is often referred to as an attachment disorder, where a child wants to bond but the pain of the anticipated rejection makes the bonding too scary; to avoid the pain of separation, they avoid attaching altogether. It is common in children who experience multiple losses of a caregiver.

A mother whose body is warm and smells sweet, and who offers warm milk when it is needed, leads to a baby who has a deep-seated belief that everything will be all right with the world. A baby who experiences separation or rigid care that negates their needs will become anxious and less likely to articulate these needs at all.

Trust is built and earned over time. Babies develop much of their receptive language (what they understand) in the first year of life, so do not be surprised if your eight-month old-baby gets excited when you talk about going to the park. Equally, you should avoid lying to your baby, even if you think they can't understand what you are saying.

Lying to your baby or child will lead to mistrust and resentment:

- Do not sneak out the house or lie and say, 'I won't be long,' when you are planning to be gone for the day.
- Do not sneak out after putting your baby to sleep – let them know where you plan to spend the night.
- If a medicine tastes awful, say, 'This medicine does not taste nice but you can have a sip of juice once you have taken it.' Don't lie and say it's delicious when it's not. Your baby will start refusing to take anything, unsure of what's coming.
- If an injection or vaccination is going to be sore, tell your baby, 'This will be sore, but I will be here with you and we will get through it together.'

Trust is most often built through suffering together. Rather cry alongside your baby than leave them in their hour of need, no matter how hard it is for you to watch.

Sharing joy

A secure attachment plus trust leads to the ability to share joy or have a good time together. Many parents ask me for advice regarding discipline strategies. Before you can start disciplining your baby or child, you need to create a joy-filled home. Most discipline strategies fail completely if your baby or child does not want to restore their relationship with you and rejoin the family after the punishment they receive!

What if I told you that your baby knows when you are really having fun, and benefits hugely when they are part of the action? Research by the World Association for Infant Mental Health suggests that keeping your baby out of the principal's office, and jail, could come down to a few seconds of eye contact, a smile and maybe even a good laugh shared between a mama and baba ever so often.

They call these interactions 'shared pleasure'. The more moments of shared pleasure, the healthier and happier the baby and, wait for it, the happier and healthier the mother and father! One or two of these moments per day is 'good enough'. In fact, the evidence showed that babies who have regular and joyful interactions with their mothers are more likely to go on to have regular and joyful relationships at school with their friends and even later with their life partners. On the other hand, longitudinal studies documented in a *Brain and Mind* article by Bruce Perry have shown that a child's ability to form and maintain healthy relationships throughout life may be significantly impaired by having an insecure attachment to a primary caregiver.

Initial research in mice, documented in a journal article called 'Variations in maternal care in the rat as a mediating influence for the effects of environment on development', has shown that (related and unrelated) mice put in the care of loving mothers (who are attentive and lick them caringly) grow up to be better mothers themselves when they have pups. This effect is so strong that it can even stretch over two generations, with granddaughter mice being better mothers and better able to cope with stress, too, all because their grandmother took good care of their mother. These long-lasting benefits of good parenting in mice are dependent on chemical changes in their DNA.

With love, the 'use it or lose it' principle applies. If you receive love and care, certain areas of your brain dedicated to human relationships grow and become interconnected. However, neglect or lack of care will lead to a different chain of events in both DNA and brain structure.

The reason your shared joy interactions appear to have such a long-lasting effect on your baby is that the loving care you have provided alters your baby's DNA and, in turn, their brain structure. Whether your baby is genetically related to you or not, your love can alter their DNA. Now that's the power of love.

It may feel like you are not doing much when you cuddle and chat to your baby, but you are altering their genetics – making them more prone to enjoying human relationships.

But don't try to fake it; your baby knows if you are not enjoying it and the ambiguity will only result in confusion. Even teeny babies know that a falsely cheerful face is different from a genuine smile and find it incredibly confusing. In fact, a fake smile makes them feel anxious. Unsure of whether you are safe and can be trusted – or unsafe and should be avoided – babies attach ambiguously. Babies like looking at and chatting to people whom they understand and can therefore trust. Let your words and your tone match your facial expression – your baby will learn to understand emotions like sadness and frustration by how you express and deal with them yourself.

Remember, the goal is not to be happy all the time. Nobody is. Do not try to channel Barney or Mary Poppins. Just be yourself.

Lyal's story

Lyal came to see me when he was five years old. His parents were highly successful entrepreneurs who had used IVF to conceive him. Since his birth, his parents had wanted him to become strong and independent, like they were.

He lived between two continents and had many stamps in his

passport. Because of the frequent travelling, he had attended at least two schools each year since he was two years old. He had no siblings and no pets. He had received the best care money could buy – from highly trained and caring nannies, who had already changed four times in his short lifetime. He was disinterested in his father and constantly asked, 'Where is my mother?'

The problem, which his parents could identify quite wisely, was: 'Lyal is clever but does not do what people ask him to. He doesn't care what anyone thinks of him.' They wanted me to help Lyal make friends and behave better socially.

The problem was that Lyal had learnt that attaching to his mother and father ended inevitably in painful separations while they were away overseas on business; when they were home, they were unable to be truly present. He had also learnt that even the most loving nanny and caring teacher would desert him after a few months. And so, from the age of about two and a half, he stopped caring. He did as he pleased. He pulled the cat's tail, he used his motorised car to break the roses, he hid away for hours where no one could find him. He pushed playmates away – quite literally.

He was lonely but he felt safe.

Helping Lyal would mean his parents giving him a greater degree of secure attachment. They needed to be more hands-on and spend time caring for his body. They needed to wash him, dress him and eat with him. This was not possible due to their busy schedules. They needed to play with him – but they could not afford to enjoy a childhood game when they needed to keep up appearances.

Ultimately, therapy failed: not because Lyal could not be a wonderful, kind, generous child, but because the steps needed to help him get there were missing and his parents could not put them in place, despite knowing consciously that they needed to do so.

Lyal's father was devastated when I reported that no amount of therapy would make him more 'sociably acceptable' unless they could support him at home. He said, 'I finally got the son I always wanted. I paid over R100 000 to have him and I have given him the best money can buy and he does not give me affection, he does not want to play with me or speak to me or even come with me and my friends to the golf club.'

What he failed to recognise was that, as a father, he had not given his son affection, got down onto the floor and played games that interested Lyal, or spent time listening to him and hearing about his world. He had never taken Lyal and Lyal's friends anywhere with him.

And so he labelled this son of his 'difficult and rigid' – exactly the words I would have used to describe his parenting style.

As I said earlier, there is no skipping ahead to the good parts. If you want to raise a healthy human being who is securely attached to you, you cannot outsource parenting. You will have to put time aside to connect and care on a basic level to establish a deep feeling of belonging.

Advice for balancing parenting with a busy career

Take whatever maternity or paternity leave you are granted. You will need it. If you do not qualify for paid maternity or paternity leave and your employer has contributed towards the Unemployment Insurance Fund (UIF), then you should be eligible for partial payment of your salary.

If you are self-employed, save what you can before your baby arrives to allow you to be with your baby for at least the first four weeks. Spending time with your newborn baby is one of the best investments you can make. Try to protect what time you do have with your baby. It is okay to say no to well-meaning visitors. There will be lots of time for everyone to meet your new baby in the months to come.

When you do return to work, try to negotiate baby-friendly hours. Working from 07:00 to 16:00 may make far more sense for your family than working from 09:00 to 18:00. Work from home as much as you can. This has become far more common, and thankfully saves time spent commuting.

If you are working and short on time with your baby, think about whether there is any way you could outsource activities that take you away from them (like grocery shopping, cooking and cleaning). Try to spend the time you do have before or after work focused on your young baby, who may be asleep by 19:00. You could accept a neighbour's offer to help get groceries or ask your mom to do the laundry while you hold your baby.

Push to be home before bedtime if you can. If time in the evening is short, then prioritise the basics: eat together, bath your baby and read one story or sing one song. Even 30 minutes a day can go a long way. If you can't be home for bedtime, then be present for wake-up time and perhaps develop some early-morning rituals.

Choose to say no to weekend work commitments if you can. If the weekend is all the family time that you have in a week, you will need to treat it as a truly precious resource and try to protect it as far as possible.

Plan and take regular family holidays. Include other families if you like, but be sure to focus on building memories together.

Find the best childcare you can:

- If you are lucky enough to have a family member take care of your baby, ask them to share what your baby is up to by sending you photographs and videos. Looking at pictures of your baby can help you express milk at work.
- If you can, choose to use a day mother over a crèche. Young babies need intense, focused care and a crèche filled with many young babies who all need lots of attention is not ideal. A day mother should have only a few babies in her care at any one time. Remember, your baby needs a high-quality person to love them, not a childcare centre filled with great toys.
- If you are able to hire a nanny, ask that they focus on your baby rather than on the housekeeping. However, you can't pay anyone to do for your child what you will do for free. A baby with a nanny will still need mom and dad in their life. Primary attachment should be to a parent and not to an employee who could resign at any point.

Find the support you need to be a good parent. As a career-loving parent you will need to find your tribe: the handful of people who have you and your baby's best interests at heart, as you do theirs. Remember, you are not raising your baby alone – even if you feel lonely.

USEFUL ACTIVITIES

Rather than buying into the idea that there is one perfect routine that you should be enforcing, here are some family activities that will help you decide which rhythm is perfect for your family.

Define success for your family

A good place to start as a new parent is to ask yourself:
- For me and my family, what would success look like?

- At my child's 21st birthday, what would be a sign that we did a good job as parents?
- Which values or world views do we hope to instil in this little person by the time they are a big person?

Write down what your end point looks like. It is easier to do the hard stuff in the short term if you know where you are aiming to end up in the long term. If you and your partner can agree on this goal, it will help to make all the little decisions move somewhere closer to this end point.

What it also does is help you to let go of certain 'results' that you may be clinging to or hoping for.

You will realise that a happy marriage is more important than others' opinions of your parenting. You will realise that a baby who trusts their parents may be healthier and better adjusted than a baby who is seen as successful just because they can sleep in their own bed through the night.

Practise 'oneness'

Be intentional over the course of the pregnancy, as well as after the birth. For instance, during the pregnancy you can talk to your baby, play them some music and even start reading them a bedtime story. After the birth, if the normal bonding process is interrupted for any reason then skin-to-skin contact can be used therapeutically once both parents and baby are well enough to establish the closeness needed for bonding to occur.

If you have adopted a baby, it's not too late: start your journey with skin-to-skin time and try to find times during the day where you can foster 'oneness'. Wearing your baby in a sling or enjoying nursery rhymes like 'Round and round the garden' are a great way to start. You will figure out your own family favourites soon enough!

Remember, this period of 'oneness' is a relatively short phase in the greater scheme of things. Babies should start to separate from their parents between six and nine months as their mobility increases. A baby will begin to experience separation anxiety – a sudden realisation that they are apart from their parent and that they and/or their parent could leave and choose not to return at any time. However, babies who experience small separations that end with their parent returning and meeting their needs soon graduate from this phase.

To help your baby work through their separation anxiety, play peek-a-boo and hide and seek. As they practise watching you appear and disappear, they learn that, when you go, you do come back.

Share the joy

Make it your goal to experience one moment of shared joy each day. This moment only has to last a mere five seconds, which should be very reassuring for busy parents who battle to schedule in a playtime.

As wonderful as it is to give your baby the gift of your undivided attention, it may not be feasible for some families or for some babies to play every day from 17:00 to 18:00. You cannot force the fun.

Try to build in some playful interactions during at least one of the everyday activities that you enjoy doing with your baby:

- This could be during bathing, or a silly way in which you choose to put on your baby's pyjamas.
- It could be dancing while you are cooking.
- Sing a special nursery rhyme that you all think is hilarious before bed.
- It could be the way you greet your baby each morning with a kiss.
- Or it could be how you choose to pick a few flowers on weekends for the dinner table.

On the other hand, some everyday activities that now form part of the modern parenting journey will make it more difficult for you to achieve shared joy. You won't be able to share joy if your baby can't make eye contact with you. This happens when:

- You are driving and they are in a rear-facing car seat
- You are in the shops pushing them around in a forward-facing pram
- You are walking and carrying your baby facing forward on your chest or behind you on your back
- You are watching television or working on a laptop
- You are filming or photographing your baby on your smartphone.

Be mindful of finding a way to connect regularly if you are a busy parent on the go.

Remember, shared joy requires your undivided attention, and the discipline not to interrupt the fun in order to record it. Don't spoil the fun for fear of not capturing the moment. Your baby will have more fun and laugh more often the more present you are and the more you laugh along with them. Resist the temptation to capture every moment; live the joy, instead of recording it.

REALITY 3: There is no such thing as the perfect routine

- The Unicorn Baby is easily moulded and will comply with whatever routine you choose. Your baby probably will not. And that's okay.
- There is no such thing as the perfect routine, but together you and your baby will find a flexible routine that is perfect for you.
- Instead of aiming to control when your baby feeds, sleeps and plays, focus on regular bonding, building trust and sharing joy.
- Infancy is a crucial time for brain development. How your baby is cared for will change their DNA and brain structure.

Focus on regular bonding

- Both babies and parents need to be supported during the first year to promote attachment. Accept whatever help is offered to you so you can find time to bond with your baby.
- Children who have secure attachment are likely to grow up to become happy, independent and resilient adults.

Signs that you are busting Myth 3

✔ Your baby likes you: they fall asleep on your body and calm down at the sound of your voice.

✔ When your baby is upset and sees your face, they calm down briefly and change the tone of their cry.

✔ Your baby loves smiling at you.

✔ You can list a few activities that you love doing with your baby, and that your partner loves doing with your baby.

✔ From when your baby is about eight months old, you may have become their favourite person. They know who you are and are less happy to be in the arms of strangers. This is a good sign, but it may make it harder for you to pop out to run a solo errand. Your baby wants to be with you day and night.

✔ Your baby is curious to explore away from you once they become mobile as they are confident that you will come to the rescue should they encounter trouble.

Myth 4
Breastfeeding comes naturally

Feeding the Unicorn Baby is a dream. The Unicorn Baby latches gently and stays latched for the entire duration of a feed, which is not very long, of course. They do not require any positioning or handling, so you can feed them just about anywhere. Breastfeeding a Unicorn Baby is like going on a beautiful journey filled with warmth and love. They get the amount they need and are happy to alternate breasts according to your wishes.

Breastfeeding is a natural process. Women are built biologically to produce milk. We have all the equipment necessary. However, every athlete knows that you can have 'all the gear and no idea'. Breastfeeding, like playing any sport, is an acquired skill. It takes learning and practice over time to become proficient. Unfortunately, many Western mothers may never have had an opportunity to learn from and watch other women breastfeeding before they try to breastfeed their own babies. The only images of breastfeeding you have seen are probably on the covers of baby magazines at your grocery store.

According to UNICEF, in developed countries like the United Kingdom, only 20 per cent of women are still breastfeeding when their babies are six weeks old. In developing countries like South Africa, the rate is higher – however, only one third of babies are still breastfeeding by six months. Why is it that for so many mothers breastfeeding stops being a good option?

Recently, in Milan, Italy, 273 first-time mothers with healthy, full-term babies who were exclusively breastfeeding on discharge from hospital were surveyed about their emotional experiences of breastfeeding through an online questionnaire when their babies were three months old. Surprisingly 85 per cent of the mothers reported that their breastfeeding experience was different from what they would have expected!

The reasons they listed were as follows:

- 50 per cent reported that breastfeeding had been more difficult and complex than they had expected it to be.
- 8 per cent reported experiencing unanticipated pain during breastfeeding.
- 11 per cent reported being surprised that breastfeeding had failed altogether.
- 25 per cent of the mothers reported that they found breastfeeding to be a much more positive experience than they had expected.

It is clear that, when it comes to breastfeeding, our expectations may be at odds with reality. Let's look more closely at the process of breastfeeding a newborn baby.

The breastfeeding journey

The start of your breastfeeding journey could be magic. All having gone well in the delivery, you give your first feed just after meeting your baby for the first time. And meeting your baby is an amazing experience – I would rank meeting my babies as the best moments of my life, as would most parents I know. But trying to help your baby find a way to latch (that does not cause you any pain) can be less awesome.

This is because as a mother you may want your baby to latch so badly that, even if this latch is more painful than your birth experience, you are going to grin and bear it rather than ask for some help. Many will have a look and give their opinion. Yes, suddenly everyone is checking out your breasts and nipples like they were a pair of shoes: 'Great colour areola – not sure about the length of the nipple, though. Hmmm . . . are your breasts perhaps too full for the baby to latch?' Try not to hold on to any of these proclamations too tightly.

The most important opinion is, actually, yours. Are *you* comfortable while feeding? Are *you* enjoying the experience? This seems selfish, but ultimately the maker of the milk needs to feel comfortable and relaxed to, well, make the milk.

The most common error that new moms make is not admitting that something feels off or painful. The second most common error is thinking that the next feed will be as painful as the last. Finding a good latch is usually a slow transition from getting it wrong most of the time to getting it right more of the time. Neither anticipating that it will be wonderful nor anticipating that it will be awful assures success. Breastfeeding does not always feel as you anticipated it would, and that's okay. It is really hard work, even when it is going right. Some moms feel great after breastfeeding for a few days. Others may need a few weeks or even months to get there. Some may never get there, and that's okay too.

Many moms who have breastfed for years will tell you how tough their beginning was. Breastfeeding can come naturally, but for most it does not. The beginning does not predict the outcome. For most moms, it requires some patience and lots of perseverance – even more so for mothers who have not grown up seeing other women breastfeeding. How do you learn to do something you have never seen done?

An honest heart-to-heart with another new(ish) mom or seeing a lactation consultant can help you normalise the initial awkwardness that can accompany breastfeeding. New moms are a great resource, as they are in the trenches too. Lactation consultants are often nursing sisters who are great at problem-solving to help you get a better latch and minimise the pain you may be experiencing.

If you want to breastfeed and don't feel comfortable with others watching, I suggest you opt for as few visitors as possible after your birth. This will give you and your baby a chance to figure out this latching business while you are still in hospital and have help on hand. This is because when babies want to latch, they want to latch now. Not after your sister's boyfriend leaves the room. Or your step-uncle finishes taking photographs. If you miss the moment, it is almost impossible to latch an angry newborn. Some visitors will be more important to you than others. Pick the ones who love you the most and who will understand if you stop the conversation to try to latch.

Give your nipples some love

After the birth, the priority is skin-to-skin contact. Then, once you both feel up to it, the goal is to give your baby a chance to latch.

You will be delighted and probably quite shocked at what a strong suck a healthy newborn can have. Little piranhas, they are.

It is really hard, as a new mom, to remove your sleeping, brand-new baby from your breast. You are often just too happy that they got on there at all (after trying the many, many different positions with a team of advisors on hand). Even if you and your baby have mastered latching, you could damage your nipples if you leave your baby on your breast unnecessarily for long stretches.

To help make breastfeeding wonderful for you both, you need to distinguish between feeding, soothing and 'this serves no purpose, now let me get you off my nipple so it can rest until you need it next time'.

After each feed, it is helpful to wipe your nipple with sterile or saline water and pat it dry. Leave it to hang out in a sunny spot (if you can) so that it can thoroughly dry and anything nasty can die. You can apply some lanolin oil to create a barrier just before your next feed, but try to give your nipples as much air time as possible.

If it's hot, you will need to change sweaty breast pads and maternity bras more often to avoid moist nipples that are prone to evolving into cracked and bleeding ones very quickly. As many as 80 per cent of women experience cracked or painful nipples when initiating breastfeeding. If you cannot access fresh air and sunshine, then low-level laser therapy (LLLT) may be required to reduce pain and speed up wound healing. LLLT is silent and painless. It is covered by medical aid for inpatients in private hospitals. Once discharged from hospital, you can visit a lactation consultant or physiotherapist to access it.

If your nipples are sore or your baby is struggling to latch, you can express your first milk, known as colostrum, onto your finger. Colostrum is known as liquid gold as it is so densely packed with calories and antibodies. It is sticky and probably most similar in consistency to honey. A baby needs only a few drops to feel satisfied. Press on the areola (dark area around your nipple) to release the colostrum. Yes, you are milking yourself, and yes, it is amazing.

If your baby is finished feeding but just loves sucking, you can offer them one of your fingers or a dummy to suck instead of your nipples. It is also helpful to pick a side for each feed. Let your baby suck on the left breast this time and the right one next time. This gives each nipple a few hours off to heal.

If you or your baby develop an itchy or painful red rash punctuated with white dots, you could have thrush. Thrush is an overgrowth of naturally occurring yeasts. It is common in a baby's mouth (it looks like milk deposits, but does not come off when you rub it) and digestive tract (it can lead to a sore throat and sore tummy), and on their bottom (it often looks like a nappy rash). It can also be found on a mother's nipples or as a vaginal yeast infection. It is very common, but can become painful for mom and baby if left untreated. Tell your pharmacist if you suspect that you or your baby have thrush as you will need to be treated at the same time to avoid re-infecting each other.

The worst day of your life

Shortly after giving birth, you will be told not to worry if you cry a lot on the day your milk comes in. The joke is that no one can tell you what day exactly this will be. It is usually around day two to five after giving birth that your gold colostrum starts to become milkier. You will feel emotionally awful in the hours before this happens, which means you will not be sure whether you are about to make milk or whether you have lost all joy forever.

You see, an unfortunate side effect of this miraculous milk-making business is a very bad day for the milk-maker. Making breast milk involves an array of hormonal changes. Prolactin is a hormone involved in milk letdown that also causes dopamine levels (the happy hormone we love) to plummet. Add to this dopamine drop the fact that you are recovering from giving birth, and haven't slept well in a few days, and you may just find yourself crying for no apparent reason when your best friend brings you flowers.

I would describe my milk-coming-in experience as the back-to-school blues, or maybe like when you got your period as a teenager and suddenly everyone made you cry, for so many reasons and no reason at all. I needed lots of tea and understanding.

This day of feeling very sore emotionally will likely coincide with having very sore boobs. Before this day, all going well, your nipples may have felt only a bit tender. (All going unwell, your nipples may now be bleeding with each feed – true story.) However, your milk coming in is a different kind of discomfort. Your boobs may become enlarged and swollen and hot. This is known as engorgement. You will need to relieve the pressure and may not be able to rely solely on your baby's feeding to do this. If milk stays for too long in the breast, it goes off and may cause an infection called mastitis (inflammation of the milk glands), so you need to release the pressure.

There are many ways to reduce the pain that comes from this fullness. Some suggest using cabbage leaves. Others say a hot shower with some manual drainage to relieve the pressure is great (this involves squeezing one breast at a time with both hands to try to relieve the milk glands). Others suggest drinking some beer or champagne to help with letdown (the milk trickling or shooting out of your nipple). Others still suggest using a breast pump to clear each and every duct (in case your baby has missed a few zones during a feed).

Because babies often have preferences, your cherub may only want to feed off one of your breasts and constantly fuss on the less-favoured side. If you can, ask your mother which of her breasts you impacted more. She probably has a story for you about her poor right boob!

Other babies may prefer a certain way of being held to feed, such as the rugby ball or the tummy-to-tummy hold. This may mean that they do not suck in all the milk from each milk gland, leaving some knobbly, swollen zones. These zones, which feel like chewing gum under your skin, are full milk glands . Identifying and emptying them is essential so that they do not get blocked.

Don't cry over spilt milk

When you are relieving engorgement, letting some milk spill in the shower or into your lap is not a problem. Your body will make more. Just as you needed to protect your nipples in the first few hours and days of feeding, you will need to look after your boobs to have a successful breastfeeding journey. Severe mastitis may result in scarred milk glands that can no longer produce milk, so make checking and massaging your breasts a regular self-care practice in the first few days and weeks of breastfeeding.

Figure out what works best for your breasts. I do, however, warn against over-pumping with a double pump (both breasts at the same time) – because breastfeeding works on the supply-and-demand principle, this will lead to your making more milk. This can be a blessing and a curse. Lots of milk is great for baby, but it can mean that you have to keep up the pumping to prevent engorgement.

The most common things that get in the way of breastfeeding

There are many reasons why breastfeeding may not go well. This list is far from exhaustive. La Leche League International is a non-governmental non-profit organisation that organises advocacy, education and training related to breastfeeding. It has a presence in about 89 countries. You can visit their website (www.llli.org) for sage breastfeeding advice.

My hope is that you encounter no obstacles at all, and that it is easy for you from the first feed. However, if you are among the overwhelming majority and your breastfeeding journey does not start like this, here are some common obstacles to consider.

Physical obstacles

There are many anatomical issues that can make breastfeeding difficult. Let's play a little game of true and false to see what they are.

1. **You cannot breastfeed if your breasts are small.** This is false. Breast size is not an indicator of your ability or inability to breastfeed. Breast size is mostly due to fatty tissue, and fat does not make milk. A woman's milk glands and ducts develop during pregnancy, and it is this bit of the boob that is important for breastfeeding.

2. **If you have had a surgical procedure done to your breasts, you won't be able to make enough milk.** This is mostly true. If your glandular tissue has been damaged during breast surgery, exclusive breastfeeding can be difficult. Some women have battled cancer. Others have opted to have a double mastectomy due to carrying a breast cancer gene. Others still have needed breast reduction surgery, or opted to have breast enlargement surgery.

   If you have undergone one of these procedures, then your chance of being able to produce milk will vary:

Double mastectomy   Very low chance, as no glandular tissue remains

Breast reduction   Very low chance if nipples were moved in surgery; better chance if the surgery was less invasive

Breast enlargement   Lower chance if implant is on top of muscle; higher chance if implant is behind muscle

If you are uncertain how much of your glandular tissue has been affected, I encourage you to initiate breastfeeding and give your baby colostrum – and later, if possible, some breast milk. Every day of breastfeeding is helpful, so try not to decide too much ahead of time. If it becomes clear that you don't have the milk glands necessary to make enough milk for your baby, it is easy enough to start top-up feeding.

   If you know you will be bottle feeding, then focus on

skin-to-skin contact and make feeds a special time for you and your baby. Look for your baby's hunger cues and respond as you would if you were breastfeeding.

3. **You cannot breastfeed if you have flat nipples.** This is false. Babies should latch onto the areola (the dark area around the nipple) with the nipple all the way at the back of their mouths. If your nipples don't stick out much, your baby should still be able to latch onto your breast and get milk from you. Some moms have reported using a breast pump to suction their breast and nipple into a more conical shape before offering it to their baby. Others have used nipple shields to create the shape they need. If you are worried about the shape of your nipples, try one of these techniques. Speak to an experienced nursing sister or a lactation consultant if you have any anxieties about the shape of your breasts or nipples.

Remember, as breastfeeding continues your breast and nipples will change shape dramatically anyway to fulfil their function. This is amazing – but rest assured, your nipples will not stay as dark or as long as they will be during the early days of breastfeeding. The body adjusts and re-adjusts as needed, so beautifully. No, you won't get your pre-baby boobs back (back is gone, remember?) but you won't be stuck with the boobs you have at the beginning of your breastfeeding journey either. This may be good or bad news for you, depending on your love for big boobs.

4. **You cannot breastfeed a premature baby.** This is both true and false. Some premature babies can suck better than others. Girls usually suck better than boys. Older babies usually suck better than younger babies. And some premature babies surprise everyone in the NICU. A baby usually develops their suck-swallow-breathe (SSB) reflex by the gestational age of 36 weeks old. But GA is not everything. Your baby's GA is based on your menstrual cycle and, as such, is not always 100 per cent accurate. Your baby may be slightly younger or older than thought, and may not have developed the SSB reflex at this stage.

5. **A tongue tie or lip tie can make breastfeeding sore.** This is true. While mild tongue ties or lip ties may not cause any feeding issues at all, those who have tried to breastfeed a baby with a moderate or severe tongue or lip tie will tell you how painful and impossible it is. You are probably thinking, *A what tie?* I had no idea these even existed either until I had my own baby. Let's have a quick look at what they are.

   Tongue ties and lip ties are simple midline deformities or oral tethers. They occur in the middle of the body and can range from mild to severe in nature.

   In a tongue tie, the membrane that holds the tongue in place is overgrown. This means that you cannot run your finger around the inside of your baby's bottom jaw (along where the back of the bottom front teeth would be). The membrane holds the tongue down, making it relatively shorter. The baby has trouble sticking out their tongue. This may negatively impact the tongue's ability to move like a wave as it milks the breast. It can also make swallowing more tiring. Besides having an effect on feeding, tongue ties are also linked long-term to difficulty with oral hygiene, articulation and even French kissing!

In a lip tie, the membrane that controls the top lip is overgrown. This means you cannot run your finger along the front of your baby's top tooth line. The membrane holds the top lip down onto the gum. This makes it difficult for your baby to 'clear' their top lip and place it above your areola during latching. The top lip curls in, instead of curling up, when latched. This may negatively affect breast-feeding if the baby cannot make a seal with their lips or create negative pressure after latching. Your baby may not stay latched for long, and feeding will be more tiresome. A lip tie has fewer long-term difficulties but may result in a noticeable gap between the front teeth once they grow in.

If you suspect a tongue or lip tie, speak to a healthcare professional while you are still in hospital. They will be able to refer you (if appropriate) to a paediatric dentist or ear, nose and throat surgeon to assist with getting it snipped if you wish to continue breastfeeding. Simple tongue ties and lip ties that do not have blood supply are easily snipped. However, more complex ties require more intricate surgery.

Some parents opt to wait until their baby is older. This may seem sensible and could be the right choice for your family, but your baby needs to develop their lip and jaw movements in the first year to support speech production and manage solids. Early intervention is linked to more positive outcomes. Research has shown that there can be a benefit in terms of a baby's weight gain, less nipple pain for the mother, and an increased chance of continued breast-feeding.

In my experience, because the membrane thickens as the child grows older, the surgery required is often more intricate and requires more aftercare. This appears to be handled better by a sleepy baby than it is by a busier toddler or preschooler who wants to eat solids and talk. Ultimately, the choice is yours.

Socioemotional obstacles

The reasons why many mothers do not breastfeed, or give up breast-feeding, are often surprisingly complex and deeply personal. It is every mother's right to choose how to feed her baby. She does not have to explain her decision, despite being asked about it incessantly. Social boundaries do seem to fade after having a baby, so you should anticipate that the cashier is going to ask you, 'Why is your baby drinking a bottle of formula?' Unsolicited questioning by strangers is probably the only downside to becoming a member of the worldwide parenting community.

Here are the less visible obstacles to breastfeeding that I have encountered in my practice:

1. I don't want to breastfeed for too long as I don't want to ruin my boobs forever.
2. My partner thinks it's weird and doesn't like it.
3. I want to get back on to contraceptives. I can't risk falling pregnant again.
4. The idea of a person (even a small person) demanding to touch my body triggers me.
5. I want to get my libido back – breastfeeding has killed my sex life and I miss it.

6. Breastfeeding makes me feel heavier than I want to. I have had eating disorders in the past and I am afraid I will relapse if my breasts remain this huge.

7. I gave up alcohol for nine months. I just don't want to carry on without being able to drink.

8. I know I have to go back to work soon and want to be sure my baby is able to bottle feed. I don't want to worry about them being hungry when I'm not home.

9. I need to take chronic medications that I know could be harmful to my baby.

Whichever obstacles you may encounter, please remember the best way to feed your baby is to feed your baby. You decide what milk your baby drinks and your baby chooses everything else – how fast they drink, how often they drink, and how long they drink for.

We will discuss this idea more as we look at the next myth in the next chapter: You should only feed your baby every four hours.

My story: Why I hate breastfeeding

While most moms-to-be spend months dreading their baby's exit strategy, I spent my second pregnancy dreading what would come after our baby was put on my chest. You see, I would rather do 20 hours of labour, without drugs, than breastfeed. Here's why.

I hate breastfeeding because it is so darn hard

Yup, I said *hard*. It's not natural and it's not lovely, for most. Breastfeeding your baby on demand can feel like well-thought-out torture. Some make it look black-and-white-photo fabulous; my experience has been similar to the first time you have sex. In the beginning you feel awkward. You don't know where to put your hands, and find it mind-bogglingly messy. But as time goes on, you both get better at it and land up having a wonderful time.

At its worst, breastfeeding can be excruciatingly painful (cracked and bleeding nipples anyone?); at its best, it is an intimate bonding time (those gorgeous pouty lips that stare back from the milk coma). But, and I'll be honest here, feeding your infant over and over again is tedious. Eight to 12 feeds per day can easily take 3 to 6 hours, depending on your baby's ability to guzzle. That's a big portion of the day to sit still!

I hate breastfeeding because it's so mysterious

How does a drink of cloudy water make a baby grow so rapidly? A baby doubles their birth weight on breast milk alone in the first six months, and continues to grow – with breast milk as their main source of nutrition – until the end of the first year, when solids take the lead.

Human milk is best for human babies, but the downside is that you will never know how much your baby has drunk. You won't know what the composition of your milk was. You won't be able to tell the clinic sister that your baby takes 100 ml every three hours. You will have to trust your maternal instincts (and that your baby is outgrowing their clothes). This is not easy. I prefer numbers, stats and charts.

I hate breastfeeding because everyone tells you that bottle feeding is so much better

But when you finally make the switch, hoping for some 'easier' in your routine, you realise that there is no 'easier'. Getting the temperature just right or dealing with stinkier nappies sucks. Plus, there is no perfect formula, just like there's no perfect partner (another one of life's surprises). But once you try them out you will likely get stuck with the one that suits your baby's constitution. This will be the same formula that costs the GDP of a small country. That's just how it works. Take the boob away and your baby will punish you by expressing their expensive taste.

Which brings me to expressing breast milk. Marketed as the modern women's cure-all, expressing is everything I hate about breastfeeding minus the cute baby. It's great that you get a 'bottle of freedom' but in reality it's noisy, can hurt, and makes for tons of extra washing up and sterilising ('cause you really needed some more housework, with all that free time you now have). Not to mention its power to make you feel like a brainless cow. Repeat after me: 'I am a super-powerful maker of milk, not a dairy cow.'

I hate breastfeeding because it's so messy

In case you haven't seen it, breastfeeding is not a slow trickle from one hole in the middle of your nipple (this took me by surprise too). It's closer to turning on a sprinkler system. Milk letdown means 9 to 15 jets of milk that can spray an impressive distance across a room, or at least make a wet patch on your fresh outfit. Add to the regular boob showers a baby who coughs up, possets and vom-bombs, and you're going to find yourself in a state of varying dampness for at least a few months.

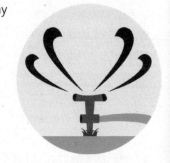

I hate breastfeeding because it invites stares

Your child is fussing. Folks are looking and now you need to whip out your noombies under a cloth that renders you blind to what is happening beneath.

Because life happens and most of the time (especially with a second or third child) you won't be feeding in your rocking chair in the dim light of the nursery, you'll be trying to feed under your jersey, in your car, while waiting to fetch your toddler from school. Or at the shops with your baby in a sling attached to one boob while shopping for groceries . You see, kids do not always follow the clock and they do not seem to care how embarrassed you may feel. Yes, you can 'free the nipple', but sometimes you just want to feed your baby without engaging in public discourse.

I hate breastfeeding because it's so unglamourous

When I am breastfeeding I get so tired of clothes that open at the front. Oh, to wear a dress, polo neck or slip-on anything. Breastfeeding is all about easy access. This means feeding bras (yuck), feeding tops (you need to learn to operate clasps with one hand at lightning speed) and milk-absorbing breast pads.

I rebelled, once, against this prescriptive wardrobe. I wore a backless, high-neck floral dress to a mate's wedding when my first baby was four and a half months old. No bra, no breast pads, I was loving life until I had to remove the entire dress to feed in the nude! And let's just say that dancing was off the cards. Don't do it. You need the gear. Rather find a nursing or maternity brand that you love and spoil yourself with functional clothing that makes you smile. There are some glorious options out there.

I hate breastfeeding because it makes you so darn hungry

I become as hungry as a teenage boy going through a growth spurt in winter. I can't seem to eat enough before my body shouts: 'More water, more fat, more protein! Now!' My body is not satisfied with a biscuit or a slice of toast. It wants real food. Meat, potatoes and vegetables at 10 p.m.? Full-cream yoghurt at 4 a.m.? Body, are you for real? You see, breastfeeding burns the same calories as a 5 km run . . . daily. The hunger *will* find you.

I hate breastfeeding because it's so unsexy

Sex sells, so that makes breasts . . . big money! But strangely, using them for their intended purpose (I am talking about breastfeeding here) makes them seem less desirable, less socially acceptable and less feminine. It's a bizarre world we live in. Ironically, though, for many of us ladies it's the only time in our lives that we have an astounding, taut bosom and enviable cleavage. Wouldn't it be great if we could claim back the breast as a source of love, warmth and nourishment? And whip it out unashamedly when we need to feed our hungry babies? #breastfeedingisbeautiful.

But most of all I hate breastfeeding because it's just so good for your baby

This means that, even if it is the hardest thing you have ever done, seems to make no sense, leaves you messy and exhausted and feeling as sexy as a cow, and gives you the munchies at 4 a.m., you will just keep doing it. One feed at a time, one day at a time, until your baby suddenly doesn't want to any more. And then, after you've resented it for so long, it will be gone and you will miss it.

If you wanted to breastfeed and it did not work out for your family, give yourself a chance to feel the disappointment. Remember, at 21 years old your child is not going to remember how long you breastfed them for – but they will remember how you made them feel. So make feeding a special way of showing love, in whatever form it takes.

REALITY 4: Breastfeeding is hard work and may be very different from what you expected

- The start of your breastfeeding journey could be magic. It could also be less magical than you hoped. A bad start does not mean you're doomed to fail.

- You will need to let go of any proclamations that others have made about your body, breasts or nipples. They will not serve you well.

- You will need to find a way to feed your baby that is comfortable for you and your baby. You will be spending a lot of time feeding in the first few months, so think carefully about where you would like to feed.

- If you are breastfeeding, you need to look after your nipples and breasts. Show them some love.

- Being aware of the obstacles that you and your baby may face can help you to understand why many struggle to breastfeed.

- Making peace with how you end up feeding your baby is important. The most important thing is that you and your baby are happy and healthy. The parenting road will be far longer than your breastfeeding journey.

> A bad start does not mean you're doomed to fail

Signs that you are busting Myth 4

✔ You recognise that breastfeeding is hard work.

✔ You see breastfeeding as a new skill and know it will take time to learn how to do it.

✔ You know that there are resources available to help you breastfeed if you want to, such as other moms who are breastfeeding, lactation consultants and online platforms such as La Leche League International.

✔ You are aware of the many obstacles that could make breastfeeding difficult, or even impossible. Not everything will be within your control.

✔ You may not be able to breastfeed. And that's okay.

Myth 5
You should only feed your baby every four hours

The Unicorn Baby feeds for 30 minutes every four hours. They do this six times a day for the first four weeks at 06:00, 10:00, 14:00, 18:00, 22:00 and 02:00. Thereafter, of course, they drop the 02:00 night feed so their parents can sleep peacefully and deeply from 22:00 until 06:00. They are benefiting from this predictable schedule that gives them both the nutrition and rest they need. They are responding appropriately to their parents' disciplined care.

I bumped into my old friend Jennifer from varsity days, who had just had her second baby. I asked her how it was going this time around and she laughed, saying, 'We're still in that waiting-for-a-pattern-to-emerge phase. You know, that time when you're pretending that you actually have a routine but have no idea when your baby will need to feed next?'

I couldn't stop smiling at her frankness. She had spoken this reality: babies land up in a feeding routine not because we design and implement a great feeding routine from day one but because we learn from our babies what they need.

You could say *they* train *us* into implementing a routine that helps meet *their* needs.

For example:

- A baby who likes feeding in the day will feed better in the day, so you will feed them more during the day.
- A baby who prefers feeding at night will feed better at night, so you will feed them more at night.
- A baby who needs to drink smaller volumes more frequently will drink smaller volumes more frequently more happily, so you will feed them smaller meals more often.
- A baby who likes a bigger meal less often will feed for longer, less often. So you will feed them bigger meals, less often.

I am sure you can see the pattern here: what works for your baby is what you will have to do.

Let's look at some feeding terminology, as it can get rather confusing.

Scheduled feeding is feeding either at a set time, such as 13:00, 17:00 and 21:00, or at set intervals, such as every four hours. Using intervals can involve timing from the beginning of one feed to the beginning of the next feed. It can also mean timing from the end of one feed to the beginning of the next. There are many scheduled feeding programmes out there; to keep you slightly dazed and confused, they all use slightly different methodology.

Responsive feeding is also referred to as demand feeding. Feeds are given when a baby gives a hunger cue. Feeds are ended when a baby gives a fullness cue. The idea is that a hungry baby feeds better than one that is not hungry.

Cluster feeding is when a baby suddenly chooses less space between feeds and is feeding more than usual. For some babies, this happens at certain times of the day – usually the time you planned to be doing something other than feeding. Cluster feeding is a normal part of a baby's development, rather than a sign that something is wrong with your milk or your parenting.

Not all days in a baby's life are the same. On some days, there is more growth and development than others. On these days, it may seem that your baby is at the breast for a good part of three or four hours. On other days, they may stay on the breast for ages just before they go to sleep.

It is thought that cluster feeding gives your baby what they need – more milk to match their sudden growth spurt. It is also thought to prepare the mother to make a greater volume of milk going forward as the baby requires a greater volume or a different composition of milk. Remember, it's all about supply and demand when it comes to breastfeeding.

Babies who are bottle fed, using expressed breastmilk or formula, can also cluster feed. If your baby polishes off their usual bottle and is unable to settle as they seem hungry for more, simply feed them more. Put another bottle together and see what they do. If they drink more, they needed more.

There are other times in the first year when your baby is likely to cluster feed. Cluster feeding is more likely to occur:

- In the first two months of your baby's life, when your baby is growing exponentially faster than at any other time of their life
- When your baby is conquering a milestone, such as babbling, rolling or sitting up

- When your baby is getting ready to transition to solids, at four to six months
- When your baby is teething and needs to soothe their gums.

If babies all have different feeding needs, where do these four-hourly feeding schedules come from?

According to the World Health Organization, throughout much of the 20th century Western medical professionals recommended that newborns be fed on a highly regulated timetable.

This was mostly because, a hundred years ago, for the first time in human history medical men became the authority on when to feed babies, rather than the baby's parents.

Fast forward to the present, and many 'parenting gurus' have picked up the baton, prescribing highly regulated schedules for feeding and sleep. These timetables promise a lot. In the short term, they promise to make your job as a parent much easier. And while this may work for some babies, in the long term it may not be in your or your baby's best interests.

It has taken fifty years of scientific research to prove that human babies should be fed the way in which they had been fed for thousands of years before the medical men's bad advice became so popular.

Thankfully, today most of the scientific community knows better and well-informed medical men and women are using this science to advise parents more safely on feeding practices. However, despite all this evidence, sometimes a professional continues to promote their personal or cultural bias, or what they think works, rather than what we know about a baby's biology. Do not be too surprised if you are told to get your baby on to a four-hourly feeding schedule at some point in your first year.

Truth be told, there is no scientific basis for how much or how often to feed a baby because nobody knows the exact volume or feeding schedule that your baby needs. By this, I mean that there is no scientific evidence to say that your one-month-old baby must drink X volume every Y hours. There are rough guidelines, yes, but these are guidelines. Many babies may not finish this volume, and others may need more. And that is okay.

Most feeding schedules were designed around nursing staff shifts and hospital policies. In the past, it was customary for babies and their mothers to be separated after birth. Mothers slept in the maternity ward and babies went to the nursery. Hospitals are run according to rules and orders. If a doctor prescribes X amount of medicine every Y hours, it is up to the nurse to make sure it is given. If a dietitian asks for 90 ml feeds every four hours, it is up to the nurse to make it happen.

Nurses work 12-hour shifts. In this time they need to get through the nurses' rounds, the doctors' rounds, giving each patient their medication, feeding the babies, dealing with nappy changes, bathing and dressing them, and changing bed linen. It was impossible, in the past, for nursing staff to feed each baby responsively.

This hospital policy became the feeding regime that followed babies home.

Fortunately, there have been massive shifts in attitudes and understanding that have seen a new gold standard emerge. The Baby-friendly Hospital Initiative (BFHI) is a guidance document that was coordinated by the World Health Organization Department of Nutrition for Health and Development and the United Nations Children's Fund (UNICEF) Nutrition Section, Programme Division. This programme was designed to protect, promote and support breastfeeding in facilities providing maternity and newborn services.

In stark contrast to the previous way of doing things, since 1991 the BFHI has asked hospitals to follow a drastically different process post birth. This includes accommodating skin-to-skin contact immediately after delivery, allowing for rooming in (a baby and their mother stay together in the same room), and prescribing responsive feeding. These changes mean that nurses and parents should work as a team to care for a baby. It would prove to be a big shift in the power dynamic between healthcare providers and their patients.

The BFHI has been implemented in almost all countries in the world, with varying degrees of success. It was updated in 2006 specifically to address the situation of women living with HIV. It included guidelines for 'mother-friendly care' and described breastfeeding-friendly practices in other facilities and communities. Standards for providing support for 'non-breastfeeding mothers' were included, as the initiative encompasses ensuring that all mothers, regardless of feeding method, get the feeding support they need.

Unfortunately, as of 2017, only 10 per cent of infants in the world were born in a facility currently designated as 'baby friendly'. So, what happens if you don't give birth in such a hospital?

Do not panic. You and your partner can advocate to implement the Sacred Hour, keep your baby with you and feed responsively. Once you are home, if your baby is happy and healthy but wanting to feed more often than the mythical every four hours, feed your hungry baby!

What responsive feeding looks like

Feeding your baby frequently and on demand goes far beyond the first four weeks of your newborn's life. Here are the current WHO and UNICEF feeding guidelines for babies and children.

Start breastfeeding within one hour of birth

Babies who do not require medical intervention at birth should be left to experience skin-to-skin contact on their mother's chest in the Sacred Hour. This time together helps the baby locate and latch onto the nipple. The baby's suck stimulates the release of colostrum.

Colostrum helps a baby transition from receiving nutrition from their umbilical cord to drinking breastmilk. For a few days, the colostrum helps to flush out the meconium that lines the baby's gut (a mix of dead gut cells and digestive juices), causing your baby to make crazy black tar poos. It also helps to establish a healthy gut and immune system.

By day three or four, the colostrum changes to become whiter and thinner as breast milk starts to flow. This momentous change is accomplished by a surge of powerful hormones that can leave a new mother feeling teary and hopeless. These feelings should pass as quickly as they came once your milk is in. Tell everyone to be extra nice to you when your milk is coming in – it's pretty remarkable, and you are allowed to feel more fragile than usual.

Exclusively breastfeed a baby for the first six months of life, if possible

Responsive feeding is the best way to get breastfeeding off to the right start, and a great way to keep it going. This is because of the supply-and-demand mechanism: the more a baby feeds, the more milk a mother produces. It helps you produce the right amount of breast milk for your baby or babies (ooh, the thought of feeding twins and triplets!).

It takes a few days for your milk to come in, and a few weeks for your volume to settle. Breastfeeding tends to work better when it is not disrupted, so avoid messing with the system by giving your baby water, tea, or top-up feeds between breastfeeds in the first four weeks. You can trust that your breast milk contains everything your baby needs.

Introduce nutritionally adequate and safe complementary foods at six months, together with continued breast-feeding up to two years and beyond

So many parents are uncertain about when and how to start solids. It is important to remember that, in the first year, milk is your baby's primary source of energy and nutrition. Solids offer a baby a chance to explore taste and texture, and increase their iron stores. Exposing a baby to various proteins (egg, nuts, fish, etc.) also reduces their chance of developing food allergies.

At six months, your baby is exploring solids to gain the skill base or components they need to be a good future feeder. Exploring solids before your baby truly needs to eat solids to survive is a clever way for your baby to learn these skills.

Signs that your baby is ready for solids are:

1. Your baby has head control when held in sitting.
2. They are able to push up on their arms in tummy time.
3. They have improved sitting balance.
4. They show interest in your food.
5. They are putting everything in their mouth.

Mouthing is the term we use when babies put things in their mouth. Usually, the first thing that they put in their mouth is their own hand. This causes two areas in the brain's cortex to light up: the sensory homunculus and the motor homunculus.

The outer area of the brain is known as the cortex. The cortex has both sensory and motor regions. The sensory homunculus is where every sensation is registered – it is how you know there is a stone in your shoe or a hair in your mouth. The motor homunculus is where every movement comes from. It is the reason why, when you feel the stone in your shoe, your brain sends a message for your toes to curl, or when you feel a hair in your mouth your brain sends a message to your tongue to protrude so you can try to remove it.

Can you guess which body part takes up the largest area in the sensory homunculus? And which takes up the largest area in the motor homunculus?

Clue: The answer to both questions is the same!

The body parts that take up the most area in both the sensory and the motor homunculus are the hand and the mouth (including the lips, tongue and jaw). You know this to be true because these are the areas that you feel so well – a paper cut is awful and an ulcer on your tongue is horrendous compared to a bruise on your back or a cut on your shin.

Why is so much space given to these two relatively small body parts? The answer is that these body parts need rich sensory information for them to perform intricate and varied motor patterns.

Amazingly, when your baby is mouthing, they are lighting up most of their sensorimotor cortex. It is the most stimulating thing they can do. They are learning about how their hands and mouth work together long before they will eat solid food or say their first word.

Mouthing is essential to both development and survival. Let your baby mouth their hands as much as possible. Avoid baby mittens and any positioning that may prevent them from getting their hands to their mouth.

Babies also gain a lot of information and benefits from mouthing non-food items. They should put non-food items into their mouths (such as rattles, teething rings and soft toys), as this desensitises the mouth and prepares them for eating solids and speech production. Everyday objects also carry microbes (tiny single-cell organisms such as fungi and viruses) that your baby needs to get into their gut to build resistance to disease and prevent allergies.

Use your common sense to decide which non-food items are safe, but try to let your baby experience a range of sizes and textures.

Within reason, you want your baby to be exposed to dirt (soil, pet fur, plants and grass), as this will build their immunity and help prevent childhood illnesses such as asthma further along their journey.

Continue frequent, on-demand breastfeeding until two years of age or beyond

For some, this is a very difficult task. For others, reaching this milestone happens more quickly than expected. Most mothers who are breastfeeding will cite returning to work as the greatest barrier to continued breastfeeding. Unfortunately, once back at work the stress hormones that are secreted in high-performance environments, as well as the long intervals between feeds, can cause even the most avid breastfeeder to have a dwindling supply.

Working moms who have managed to keep breastfeeding after going back to work suggest:

- Ensuring that you eat and drink regularly
- Expressing or pumping every two to three hours to keep up the demand
- Finding a space for pumping in which you feel relaxed
- Watching videos or looking at photographs of your baby while pumping
- Feeding as often as possible when reunited with your baby (for example, at night or over the weekends).

Practise responsive feeding

Interestingly, responsive feeding is not limited to the first few weeks or months of life. Responsive feeding describes feeding both infants and older children to ensure they get enough food regularly. Parents are encouraged to feed their children directly, slowly and patiently. It is recommended that they encourage their infant or child to eat, but not force them to eat more if they are full. This helps a child establish a healthy link between hunger and fullness. They eat when hungry and stop when full.

During feeding, the baby should be an active participant and not a passive recipient. Eating should involve some eye contact and a chance to talk about the food being eaten. Unfortunately, many parents use a screen as a distraction to allow them to feed their baby a bigger volume more quickly without them 'noticing'. Feeding should be a social exchange – it is about far more than just getting food in. Feeding should be fun too. It is about joining the family and enjoying eating together. Babies need to be exposed to the foods you eat and how you eat them. Eating family meals together is a crucial part of growing a healthy eater.

Practise good hygiene and proper food handling

Breastfeeding is the laziest way to achieve good hygiene as milk is produced as and when it is needed. If you feed using expressed breast milk or formula, sanitise all bottles and accessories, including dummies.

How to sterilise baby stuff:

1. Wash your hands.
2. Wash all parts with soap and water.
3. Soak in a bleach solution for five minutes OR
4. Place in boiling water for five minutes.

If your baby crinkles their nose at the smell of bleach, steaming or boiling may be a better option.

Handling solids is slightly different. Remember to wash your hands before you prepare each feed. You can steam, boil, or roast food as you prefer. Once cooked, it is wise to decant a small portion of the food that you are going to give your baby into a separate bowl. This food can be heated and the spoon that goes into your baby's mouth can touch it. If your baby is full, you will have to throw out this portion of food that has come into contact with your baby's saliva on the spoon. However, the food in the original container can be placed back in the fridge or freezer and used at a later stage.

It's always a good idea to taste your baby's meal to test that it's not too hot or cold, and to make sure that it hasn't gone off. This tasting has the added benefit of communicating to your baby that the food is safe and you too would be happy to eat it.

How to use your freezer safely:

1. Keep sterilised baby stuff in your freezer where germs can't survive. It is far better than it standing on your kitchen counter.
2. Freeze your breast milk to keep it until you need it. There are many clever storage solutions available.
3. Never freeze milk or food that has thawed.
4. You can freeze cooked food by placing it into ice trays. This allows you to remove a small portion with ease. It also allows you to mix and match different flavours to increase the variety of foods your baby is eating.

Start at six months with small amounts of food and increase quantities gradually

Initially, eating solids should be fun. Speech and SOS feeding therapist, Jenna Fisher, has a mantra for new parents: 'Wearing your food is part of eating your food.'

Just imagine how the sensory and motor cortex light up when your little one plops a bowl of porridge on their head, or rubs some apple sauce into the creases of their ears, or gets spaghetti bolognese all over their face. Feeding cannot be sterile and measured. It needs to be messy, so set up for a meal as you would for finger painting or glitter art. Assume that the new food is going to go everywhere.

Each day, your baby gets to try a new food and you get to learn which tastes and textures they like (make sure you have the camera nearby – the faces can be hilarious). Offer each flavour a few times to give your baby a chance to get used to it. There shouldn't be a goal to 'finish' a pot of food.

Most babies do well to start on root vegetables such as sweet potato and carrots. They may also love fruits such as banana, pear and apple. Porridges of rice, corn, or oats are also very popular. There is no evidence to say that avoiding 'sweet' tastes will help your baby develop a taste for a wider range of foods later in life. It is obviously beneficial for your baby to eat more whole foods than processed foods, but try to keep mealtimes relaxed rather than making them into a time of pressure and achievement. Not all babies will want to eat kale or beetroot, and that's okay.

Try to avoid labelling foods as 'good' or 'bad', and hold off on praising your baby for finishing their food. How much they eat should be in response to how hungry they are, what their body needs and how tasty the food is, instead of an attempt to keep their parents happy. We want our babies to be in touch with how their tummy is responding to the foods they eat.

Gradually increase food consistency and variety

Younger babies tend to be offered more pureed foods. Foods such as runny porridge or yoghurt require no chewing, so a baby can manage them in a similar way to the way in which they have been drinking milk. If a baby has mouthed a variety of textured non-food items, it will be easier for them to tolerate foods that have a firmer consistency and differing textures.

Jenna Fisher further advises parents to think carefully about the foods that their baby is trying. Different foods require different skills.

'Meltables' are foods that become liquid once you place them in your mouth. Think finger biscuits and wafers. Again, these are often easier for a baby to manage as they require mostly the same action used for sucking milk and eating puree.

'Chewables', on the other hand, are foods that require you to bite and chew before swallowing. They include items like whole fruits and meats. The goal is to help your baby move from meltables towards chewables. Variety is very important as it helps to prevent a baby getting stuck at eating only a handful of foods, which can cause both nutritional and digestive problems.

Jenna suggests using 'hard munchables' under supervision to help your baby learn to use lateral tongue movements that are needed when managing chewables. Hard muchables are whole foods that are given to a baby to munch but not chew or swallow – think whole broccoli florets, a whole carrot, or a large chunk of cucumber. The baby holds the hard munchable in their hand and explores it with their lips, tongue and cheeks. Hard munchables help a baby to desensitise their gag reflex, learn tongue lateralisation, practise the munching action with their jaw, develop eye–hand coordination, and relieve the discomfort of teething.

It is important to recognise that, in some cultures, babies may skip the pureed food stage completely and go straight to eating table foods off their parents' plates. In recent years, the West has followed and started practising baby-led weaning. This is a feeding approach that allows your baby to choose which solids they mouth and chew on, and eventually swallow and eat, rather than mixing up purees.

In my experience, you can interweave the two approaches. Babies can enjoy both purees and table foods. Just follow your baby's cues.

It is important to note that many parents are fearful of their baby tackling solids because of the risk of choking. There is a big difference between coughing and choking.

Coughing and gagging are a baby's way of protecting their airway and moving food away from their windpipe. This is a protective and positive response, and should be encouraged. Coughing and gagging help your baby learn how to move food and saliva to where it needs to be to chew and swallow safely. It is very common for babies to cough on solid food while they are getting the hang of things. It is a very noisy event, as the windpipe is not blocked and so air can move in and out of your baby's lungs.

Choking, on the other hand, is a dangerous and a very negative experience. Luckily, it is also incredibly rare. With choking, food blocks the airway and your baby cannot move air past the block-age. This is why choking is a silent event as no air can flow over the vocal cords. Your baby will need your help to clear their airway.

If your baby is choking (and not coughing), you can do a finger sweep inside their mouth to try to remove the blockage. If this fails, quickly tip your baby upside down to use gravity to help the food fall out. Use a firm pat or two to dislodge it if the airway is still not clear.

Learning to move food around our mouths and swallow safely

is a lifelong process and many adults will continue to make mistakes every now and again. How you respond after a coughing or choking incident is very important. Comfort your baby and adapt your feeding approach where necessary, but don't overreact by avoiding solids altogether. Go back to foods that your baby was coping well with, and enjoy those together again. You can slowly try new foods again in a day or two.

Some of the common culprits that cause choking are sliced foods that become stringy after babies mouth them, such as dried mango, red and yellow peppers, droëwors and cucumber. The advantage to giving your baby a long slice rather than a small piece is that you can more easily remove this from their mouth should you need to.

The feedback that you give your baby is also vital. If your baby coughs on apple juice after tipping the cup too quickly, give your baby feedback: 'That was too fast. Let's try it a bit more slowly.' If your baby chokes on a huge bite of bread, say, 'That was a very big bite. Let's try a smaller bite this time and see how much easier it is.' Feedback is a very important part of all learning, and learning to feed is no exception.

Increase the number of times that the child is fed solids

When your baby first starts solids when you have seen signs of readiness, you can begin with one meal early in the day. Meals that your baby tolerates well can be given later and later each day, but new foods should always be introduced in the morning. This gives you a chance to see whether your baby has an allergic response, such as a rash or cramps – making dealing with the reaction far easier than if it happens at night.

From this point onwards, six- to eight-month-olds need two to three solid meals per day, while nine- to twenty-three-month-olds need three to four solid meals per day with one to two additional snacks as required.

Use fortified complementary foods or vitamin and mineral supplements as needed

Your baby receives many essential vitamins and minerals via the placenta *in utero* and later from the milk you feed them.

One of the best-researched minerals that your baby needs is iron. Do you know where your baby gets their iron from? The answer might surprise you.

Iron is a really important mineral that is responsible for the health of our red blood cells and, ultimately, the amount of oxygen that can be carried in our blood. Having low iron levels makes it difficult to lay down memories and learn new things.

Ideally, a baby will receive enough iron from their mother during pregnancy to lay down iron stores for the first six months of their life. Mothers who smoke, or who have high blood sugar or gestational diabetes, may struggle to pass their iron via the placenta to their babies. All these risk factors result in some babies being born with an iron deficiency, which is also known as anaemia. Babies who are born prematurely may have an increased risk of developing anaemia as they have not had as long to build up these stores.

Thankfully, most pregnant mothers are closely monitored to ensure that they have enough iron to help their unborn baby get what they need. In addition, paediatricians also test at-risk babies for anaemia and initiate iron supplementation if needed.

Most babies are born with great iron stores and can happily live off this iron for the first six months of life. Yes, there are small amounts of iron in breast milk and baby formula, but a baby does not have to absorb this iron to survive. But from six months onwards, your baby will need to eat and drink foods that are rich not just in energy, but also in iron, to continue to live healthily.

A fortified cereal is any porridge that has added vitamins and minerals to ensure that if a baby eats only this popular baby food they will get what they need. However, you know how important variation is for development – so it is wise to try to give your baby more than just milk and baby porridge. Try to introduce as many fruits, veggies and proteins as you can.

Very rarely, there are babies who, despite having access to healthy foods, battle to gain weight and grow well. There is only so much volume a baby can take in, so sometimes feeding 'more' is impossible. If your nurse or dietitian suggests adding calories to your baby's milk feeds or solid feeds, you would do well to follow their advice.

It is quite a process to add calories to milk feeds if you are breastfeeding. It requires expressing your breastmilk and adding a powder such as FM 85 to increase the calories your baby is consuming.

Adding calories to solids is often far easier. You can add calories to your baby's feeds in the following ways:

- Add a teaspoon of margarine or butter to your baby's breakfast porridge.
- Add a teaspoon of olive oil or coconut oil to your baby's lunch or supper meal.
- Give your baby a spoon of flaxseed oil, which has great nutritional benefits but does need to be kept in the fridge and used within seven days of opening.

During illness, increase fluid intake, including more breastfeeding, and offer soft, favourite foods

Worldwide, more children die of diarrhoea than any other illness. These deaths are avoidable – but in many countries a parent does not have access to clean water or the necessary medicines. If you notice that your child starts vomiting or has runny stools, you will need to pay closer attention to what they are taking in and see a health professional if you become concerned that they are dehydrating.

If you are breastfeeding, continue doing so as breast milk is easily digested and your baby will receive some of your antibodies via the milk. However, if you are no longer breastfeeding or your baby is drinking formula or cow's milk, replace all feeds with a rehydration solution and offer soft favourite foods (such as apple sauce or yoghurt). This is because cow's milk is hard to break down and digest during gastrointestinal illness, but, yoghurt contains bacteria that partially digest the lactose before it is eaten. Visit your nearest clinic if your baby is unwell and is not keeping feeds in.

Here is how to create an electrolyte-rich solution for your sick baby to drink. Offer your baby small sips of this solution frequently.

1. Boil one litre of water and let it cool to room temperature.
2. Add one teaspoon of salt.
3. Add eight teaspoons of sugar.

Feeding on demand: If I don't use a clock, how will I know when to feed my baby?

Babies give some subtle and not-so-subtle feeding cues. Here is a list of hunger cues in a newborn from an organisation that specialises in baby feeding, La Leche League International:

Quiet requests, AKA subtle cues
- Eyes moving beneath eyelids
- Eyelids fluttering before they even open
- Mouth movements
- Restlessness
- Hands brought towards mouth.

Stronger requests, AKA less-subtle cues
- Increasing physical activity, such as turning the head when cheeks are touched
- Whimpering
- Squeaking.

Demands, AKA obvious cues
- Body and mouth tense
- Breathing becomes faster
- Baby starts to cry.

Signs that a baby is not hungry
- Disinterest in food – looking away from the breast, bottle or bowl
- Pushing food away
- Wanting to play
- Throwing food down onto the floor.

As you get to know your baby, you will become attuned to their movements and sounds. You may even hear a sound like 'neh neh' or 'ini ini' that, to you and your baby, means 'I am hungry.' Give yourself time to establish a happy feeding relationship. You are both new at this!

A visit from a feeding or lactation consultant can be hugely helpful in the first few days when you are trying to establish breastfeeding. If you are choosing to bottle feed, remember to mimic breastfeeding and hold your baby close to you with each feed. Do not be tempted to just place the bottle in their mouth while they lie in their cot or sit in their feeding chair. There is so much more to feeding than eating. Everyone enjoys eating more when the meal happens in a relaxed space with great company.

How do I know I am feeding my baby enough?

There are many helpful signs that your baby is getting enough milk. If you are in hospital, in the first few days the nurses will count their wees and poos. The more your baby is weeing and pooing, the more certain the nurses can be that digestion is taking place and your baby is getting the nutrients they need.

In the days that follow, your baby's poos should become more yellow and their wees should become bigger. You may notice that your baby can feed for longer before becoming drowsy, or that they can take in more milk in a shorter time. You may also notice that your baby is growing – baby clothing is getting tighter and the numbers on the scale are going up.

All these are good signs that feeding is going well.

As a new parent, demand feed your baby until you find a rhythm, then feed them roughly according to this rhythm – adjusting as you go for growth spurts, or when the days are warmer and they are thirstier and feeding less, or when they have sore gums and do not want to suck.

Sometimes your baby will want to feed purely because they want to be near you, as you may have had a busy day apart. The reality is that your baby is an individual with changing needs.

Their feeding routine will change as they grow – probably just a few days after you thought you had it waxed and wrote it down and stuck it on the fridge.

Development = transition

As with every area of development, things do not happen overnight. Instead, there is a transition period – an edging in that happens slowly, increasing until the change is permanent. Feeding development follows this same pattern.

There is waiting . . .

If you are trying to establish breastfeeding, you will wait for your milk supply to come in and then for your milk supply to settle to the right level for your baby. And then you will wait again and again over the next few months while your body adjusts to make a greater volume for your baby, who will suddenly require bigger feeds (as they grow) or smaller feeds (as they wean slowly on to solids).

Many moms will have decided to breastfeed exclusively as the benefits are well documented. As we all know, deciding and doing are entirely different things; many moms may find themselves not feeding their baby how they thought, or said, they would. And that's okay.

If you are the partner of a mother who is struggling to breast-feed, I suggest following her lead. Be supportive but don't try to fix the problem. Feeding your baby formula against your partner's wishes is not going to go down well. Breastfeeding makes a woman hungry, thirsty and prone to crying, so rather spend your time making sure there are healthy snacks, lots of cool water and plenty of tissues around.

As parents, you may decide at the beginning of your journey

to breastfeed exclusively, only to end up giving mixed feeds (a combination of breast milk and formula) for a while. Perhaps after a period of stress or illness or separation, you will go back to exclusive breastfeeding as you and your baby want to. Breast-feeding may not work out at all for your family, and you may choose to express or use formula in a bottle. Other families may choose to wean their 12-month-old baby on to cow's milk or goat's milk.

Weaning from the breast may happen far sooner or far later than you may have thought it would, which is also okay. Each baby's milk journey will look a little alike and a little different. Remember, the best way to feed a baby is to feed a baby. So, give yourself and your baby what you need to establish a healthy feeding relationship – whether that happens to be via the breast or the bottle.

What if a parent chooses to stick to the schedule and not respond to the baby's hunger cues – can a baby get used to this?

In the short term, the baby will be in a state of stress as their needs are not being met. They may give demand cues until eventually they run out of energy and fall asleep. They will not be receiving the energy they need when they need it, and will need to break down body fat to make energy until the next feed is given.

In the longer term, if their needs continue not to be met they will learn to stop giving feeding cues (as they fall on deaf ears). These babies often appear 'shut down' – a state attributed to conserving energy or 'playing dead' to survive. They may struggle to understand what their body needs as they do not develop a reliable hunger–fullness satiety mechanism. They may not truly know when they are hungry or full. Many believe that there is a strong link between scheduled feeding and why many children are battling with obesity in modern Western societies.

You can choose to enforce a strict feeding schedule, but it may not suit your baby. This will be bad for both of you. It could also lead to feeding problems when your baby grows into a child.

At my practice, I come across babies with feeding difficulties, but I also come across older children who have feeding aversions. They do not have a positive relationship with food and often cannot eat the variety of foods necessary to stay healthy. Their families are often desperate for them to eat better but do not know what to do.

Examining how they see food can reveal this common power dynamic: the parent gives the food and the baby or child eats the food. The parent is active, the baby is passive. The parent is giving, the baby is receiving. Making your baby an active participant in feeding is a positive step towards creating a healthy relationship with food. The more ways in which they can explore and discover food, the more likely they are to manage to eat the food when they are bigger.

Feeding expert Ellen Satter has a lovely way of helping parents understand what they can control and what they need to let go of. She calls this the 'division of responsibility' for feeding. She puts it this way: 'When you feed your baby, you are responsible for what your child is offered to eat: whether she will be breast- or formula fed. She is responsible for everything else: how much, how fast, how frequently.'

Your responsibilities are to:

- Choose breast or formula feeding.
- Help your baby be calm while feeding – think about what helps your baby feel calm.
- Pay attention to their sleeping, waking and feeding cues.

- Feed smoothly, paying attention to their cues about timing, tempo, frequency and volume.

So many parents create further feeding difficulties by trying to force their baby to drink at certain times, or at least drink certain volumes. Your baby is your best guide.

If a baby lives off milk, why bother with solids?

Solids may be introduced between four and seven months, but all babies rely on the milk portion of their diet to survive until they are 12 months old. Eating solids before 12 months may not be about getting energy or nutrients in, but it does have other benefits for your baby:

- It exposes your baby to new tastes and textures.
- It gives your baby a chance to practise moving food around their mouth long before they need that food to survive.
- It offers your baby a chance to practise spitting out undesired food.
- It gives your baby a chance to practise coughing as they learn to swallow food safely.
- It gives your baby a chance to engage in sensorimotor play, where they will learn more about food and their body parts.
- It helps their body learn to tolerate high-protein foods such as peanuts, eggs and fish. Babies are more likely to develop food allergies if they are not exposed to a wide variety of foods before they are nine months old.

How to help your baby explore solids

- **Show your baby where food comes from.** This can be a challenge if all your food comes ready-made in a box. Try to get your hands on whole foods so your baby can actually see you eat a whole food before they do.

- **Eat in front of, and with, your baby.** Your baby will take longer to eat a variety of foods if they are fed away from the family. A baby who is fed at the dining table while the family is eating will learn a lot from watching the other family members. Your baby will be more interested in food that they see you eating. They will also trust that something you are eating is safe and yummy.

- **Talk to your baby about how a food smells, looks and sounds when you eat it.** Certain foods look great. Others have great smells, and some make great sounds. Let your baby smell a papaya before you mash it up. Talk about how it goes from hard to soft or how juicy it can become in a blender. If you are chomping on a carrot stick, have fun trying to make a loud crunching sound with your front teeth. In doing this, you are giving your baby information about the food and clues about how to eat different foods.

- **Encourage your baby to play with their food.** Allowing your baby to play with an apple before it is pureed is a great way to help them learn more about the food they are about to eat. Likewise, giving your baby a spoon to hold to help you feed them can make feeding far more fun. Set them up to succeed at creating a real mess by doing whatever you need to do to be happy with a mess. Use a plastic feeding chair that can be hosed down or feed them outside on the grass where the mess is easier to clean up. Do not

fret if their baby porridge lands up everywhere but in their mouth – messing is part of the learning process. They will get more accurate as time goes on.

- **Show your baby what to do if they don't like the food in their mouth.** Some babies will store food that they do not want to swallow in their mouth. Others may gag or spit the food out with great gusto. Having a designated spit plate is a great way to show your baby what to do with this food. Put out a side plate for each person that is dedicated to spitting out (an important eating skill). Babies and toddlers will often be far more adventurous if they know they don't have to swallow a food that they are mouthing. Show your baby how to spit food out – into your hand or onto a spit plate. You may just have to cope with the mess while they learn how to spit it out – and, later, how to swallow it safely. As with developing any skill, they need lots of practice before they get it right.

- **Discuss how food makes our tummy feel.** You can help your baby recognise thirst by showing them that they are hot and asking them if they feel like drinking. You can also help an older baby recognise hunger by showing them that their tummy makes a rumbling sound when it empty or that they may be feeling tired because it has been a long time since they last ate. Equally, you should help them look for signs that they are full. Most babies know this very well – it is more the parents who need to learn to respect their baby when they communicate that they are full and the meal is over.

Feeding should not be a battleground – there should never be a winner or a loser. Focus on helping your baby to build a healthy relationship with food, instead of finishing a bowl of food.

My story: Breastfeeding intervals – trying to change the unchangeable

My first baby was one month old and I was told to stop feeding her so often. She was feeding every two hours for half an hour. I was exhausted. The clinic sister advised that I probably did not have enough milk. I assured her that my breasts were full – in fact, they were overflowing. She then said, 'Perhaps your milk is not rich enough for your baby. You should top up after each feed with formula and aim to feed 15 minutes later each day.'

I went to the shop and bought Stage 1 Formula. After her next breastfeed ended, I pleaded and pressed and shoved the bottle of formula into the mouth of my drowsy, full-bellied baby. She would not drink more – I could not 'top her up'.

After digesting the breast milk she woke and wanted to feed an hour and a half later. Armed with the bottle of formula, I decided to feed with that first (it was surely richer than my low-grade breast milk) and then breastfeed her later. She downed the bottle, but then refused to breastfeed. My poor breasts were raring to go . . . so while she slept, I had to pump, pump, pump (which is never as fun as it sounds).

Despite the full formula feed of 'rich' milk, she woke up an hour and a half later and wanted to feed again. Following the clinic sister's advice, I tried to push her to a longer interval between feeds. I said, 'No, no, you must wait another 15 minutes like the nurse said.' She did not seem to understand.

She wailed for 15 minutes. After all that, she could not settle on the breast. She tossed through her breastfeed – drinking between deep, sad little sobs. I had made so much work for myself – sterilising a bottle, pumping both sides and then trying to feed a flailing and wailing baby.

I learnt that day that my baby wanted to feed every two hours, whether it was formula or breast milk. So I gave up the regime and went back to breastfeeding – it required the least amount of effort for me, and I was exhausted.

At my next clinic visit I was terrified. I would have to inform the clinic sister that I had not succeeded at topping up or stretching feeds. I had failed.

Thankfully I was assigned a different nurse. She looked at me and asked, 'How often are you feeding?' I sucked the air in deep and whispered, 'Like, every two hours.' She didn't even look up, and said, 'Good. Breastfed babies need to feed eight to twelve times a day.'

That day, I learnt that babies feed more often and less predictably than the books tell you. I had felt like a failure doing eight to twelve feeds a day when I thought I was supposed to be doing six feeds a day with four-hour intervals between feeds. Meanwhile, what I had been doing was healthy and helpful.

I also learnt that, by trying to 'fix' my baby's feeding schedule and increase the intervals between the feeds, I had unintentionally made it worse for us both. As the days went on I actually felt less tired, even though I was still feeding so often. By not keeping track and not striving to meet a certain magic number, I was using less mental energy. Do what works for you and your baby, and let go of chasing the perfect number.

REALITY 5: You should practise responsive, not scheduled, feeding

- The Unicorn Baby feeds every four hours. Your baby may feed far more often than that. And that's okay.
- Babies train *us* into implementing a routine that helps meet their feeding needs, not the other way around.
- Practise responsive feeding – if your baby or toddler is hungry, you need to feed them.
- During all feeds, your baby should be an active participant, not a passive recipient.
- Feeding should not be a battleground – there should never be a winner or a loser.
- Focus on building a healthy relationship between your baby and food, instead of forcing your baby to finish a bowl or plate.
- Breastfeeding is hard. Bottle feeding is hard. Remember, hard is not wrong.

Hard
is not
wrong

Signs that you are busting Myth 5

✔ Your baby likes feeding and you enjoy feeding your baby (most of the time, anyway).

✔ Your baby is growing a little bigger each week and eating a wider variety of foods as each month goes by.

✔ Your baby is an active participant in feeding. You let them explore foods and give them feedback when they need it.

✔ You are practising responsive feeding. You feed your hungry baby and are happy to stop the meal when you see your baby has had enough.

Myth 6
You must teach your baby to sleep through the night

The Unicorn Baby does not need to be fed to fall asleep. The Unicorn Baby does not even need to be held or rocked to help them close their eyes. At largely predictable times they can simply be placed on their back in an empty cot and they will drift off to sleep gently, quickly and without any fuss. Of course, they will wake – after their naps that last exactly 90 minutes – with a smile on their face. They will wake in the morning after sleeping for a solid 12 hours. You may pick them up when you feel like it as they are always happy to play alone in their cot – cooing and giggling until you fetch them. They are self-soothers. They are contented babies. They have not been taught any bad habits by their parents, so they have developed healthy sleep associations. Their parents are getting the sleep they need to be the best parents they can be.

The baby sleep industry is booming. Parents have a problem: they are sleep deprived. They need to work and be at their best and they have a baby that keeps waking up at all hours of the night. And so every parenting expert has arrived with a foolproof sleep solution and an expensive gadget or two that will ensure that your little one falls asleep more quickly and stays asleep for longer.

You can sign up for an online course, purchase a white noise app, order noise-cancelling beanies, find cribs that rock on their own, mattresses that regulate a baby's temperature, weighted blankets that calm, and scented sleep soothers. You can buy Epsom salts for the bath, rub lavender oil on their back and give them magnesium drops.

While all these things may or may not be helpful, it is important to note that there is no miracle cure. The answer to the question, 'When will my baby sleep through the night?' is one that you might not like. While most babies are sleeping through the night by the time they are a year old, 20 per cent of babies will continue to wake at night despite various sleep training methods.

Firstly, let's look at why parents wake during the night to respond to their babies. I mean, surely if parents could get into a deep sleep they would just sleep through their baby's crying?

In Myth 3 we looked at the ideas of bonding and attachment, and touched on how bonding can change your brain. Ruth Feldman, director of the Center for Developmental Social Neuroscience at IDC Herzliya, is well known for her research into the role of oxytocin in bonding. In more recent research, she used neuroimaging and showed that oxytocin and bonding cause a structural change in parents' brains.

Pregnancy, birth and feeding were always associated with an increase in oxytocin levels but Ruth and her team found that the act of caring for a baby (handling, playing with, and dressing and bathing the baby) elicited the same oxytocin levels as seen in mothers during pregnancy, birth and breastfeeding.

Why I love this discovery is that it shows that the more a parent cares for their baby, the higher the levels of oxytocin in both the parent and the baby. This is good news for mothers who may not have had the birth experience they planned, for those who have struggled to breastfeed, for families where there is no mother present, for those who have adopted an infant, and for fathers who are the primary caregiver.

In the brain of the primary caregiver, increased oxytocin leads to the 'switching on' of the amygdala. This is a primitive area of the brain that is responsible for vigilance. Vigilance ensures survival. It is the reason why one parent may complain that they hear their baby and get up when their partner is sound asleep.

The more you care for your baby, the more you will be driven to care for them. Your amygdala will keep you alert and listening for your baby. Even more amazing? Once the amygdala is switched on, it stays on. You literally won't be able to stop thinking or worrying about your baby for the rest of your life. Your baby changes you, forever. The parenting switch is on.

So, we are biologically programmed to respond to our baby's cues. We are programmed to expect and respond to night wakings. This doesn't make the sleep disruptions any easier to bear, does it?

Secondly, let's look at why babies seem programmed to wake. Another key reason why babies are not sleeping through the night is that they are born without a circadian rhythm. Babies do not know if it is night or day.

All living creatures are governed by the 'master clock' located in the hypothalamus, but are born without connections to this area from their brainstems. While some animals, such as new-born rats, take only a few days to make this connection, it takes human babies three to four months. This means that, before the age of three to four months, there is very little any parent can do to make a baby stay asleep. The best you can do is wait until the circadian system has connected up.

But why would human babies be designed to wake up throughout the day and the night for the first three to four months? Sleeping through the night is advantageous for parents, but holds less advantages for babies. In 2014, research by professor of anthropology James McKenna showed the following:

1. **Babies who wake frequently have a higher chance of survival.** Babies who wake between sleep cycles are practising waking, a necessary survival skill as they 'check in' and maintain healthy blood oxygen levels through the night. Babies begin to breathe once the umbilical cord is cut. However it takes them some time to establish good breathing while both awake and asleep.

   Many babies 'forget' to breathe while sleeping. This is known as sleep apnoea. When it happens, a healthy baby will rouse from deep sleep into a drowsy state and take a breath. However, a baby who is finding it hard to move between sleep states may stay asleep, despite inadequate blood oxygen levels. This is obviously not a good state to be in.

   In addition, babies who complain when they are cold also have a better chance of surviving in colder temperatures than babies who do not rouse and become hypo-thermic. Babies who wake when they are hungry also prevent low blood glucose levels that can make them so drowsy that they struggle to feed.

2. **Babies who wake frequently ensure their mother produces an adequate milk supply to feed them.** These babies assist their mothers to maintain an adequate breast milk supply until six months and beyond. Because breast milk production relies on a supply and demand principle, regular night waking helps a mother's body to make more milk, which ensures that you are able to feed your baby all the milk they need now and in the months to come.

3. **Babies who wake frequently ensure that they receive the care they need to develop well.** A side effect of producing an adequate milk supply may be the delay in the return of a mother's period. A mom who is not menstruating is a mom who is less likely to get pregnant. This allows for a bigger gap between babies and keeps mom's attention focused on the one and only baby that is breastfeeding. Without competition for attention, babies get more regular contact than they would otherwise.

   Don't be fooled though: breastfeeding is not a reliable method of birth control. Talk to your gynaecologist about family planning options if you want a gap before becoming pregnant again.

4. **Babies who wake frequently get held, rocked and spoken to more often, all of which promotes their overall attachment and development in the long term.** Babies benefit from one-on-one time with their

parents, who are often more available at night than during the day.

Responsive or sensitive parenting, where a baby is picked up, fed and rocked, is associated with higher levels of oxytocin. However, a baby who becomes dependent on these comforts is seen as having 'unhealthy sleep associations'. *Say what?!* Dependence on a caregiver is the mark of failing at becoming an independent sleeper, but dependence on stuff is okay?

Why is it fine if your baby sucks a dummy or their own thumb to fall asleep, but it's not fine if they suck on your breast? Why is it okay if your baby falls asleep listening to music, but not okay if they need you to sing them to sleep? Why is it great if a baby falls asleep while swaddled or under a heavy blanket, but not great if they are falling asleep while lying in your arms?

Surely it is more unhealthy to depend on stuff than to depend on people? While some babies will happily be comforted by the stuff, others are not convinced and may want you. Is this exhausting? Yes! Is this a sign that there is a problem? No! It is a sign that they trust you.

As the La Leche League International puts it, 'night wakings are a biological norm', and not the sign of a sleep problem.

Thirdly, let's consider what is considered normal in terms of babies waking. André Fenton, professor of neurobiology at the Neurobiology of Cognition Laboratory at New York University, has been looking at the problem of night waking from another angle. He and his team have been using big data gathered from a parenting app to try to recognise when a clear sleeping pattern emerges. His hope is that parents will be able to compare their baby's sleep pattern with others to see whether what they are experiencing falls within the normal range. These patterns are described below.

Unfortunately for new parents, what his initial findings make clear is that it takes about one year for a clear feeding and sleep pattern to be established. Yup, one whole year!

At one month old, there is no clear pattern. Feeding and sleeping events are being logged randomly. Babies are feeding and sleeping as and when they need to, around the clock.

At four months old, a pattern is starting to emerge. There are now more feeding and sleep events happening in the 'day time' between 08:00 and 21:00. This could mean that babies are sleeping for longer stretches at night, but Fenton cautions that this could also be a sign that tired parents are logging fewer sleep and feeding events on their phones during the nights.

At eight months old, the pattern is becoming more established. Many babies are having consistent feeding and sleep events during the day but many are not sleeping through the night.

At one year, a clear sleeping pattern is evident. There are three separate sleep events per day:

1. Most babies are sleeping through the night.
2. Babies are napping after their morning meal.
3. Babies are napping again five hours later, in the early afternoon.

What I find interesting about this sleep research is that it shows that babies find a sleep rhythm despite living in different countries, sleeping in different environments and being cared for by different parents. It seems that napping and sleep are biologically programmed. How your baby is sleeping has more to do with their brain development and less to do with what you are or are not doing as a parent.

I know those facts are not going to comfort you at 3 a.m. when you've got up for the fourth time, but I want to make sure that you do not lose any more sleep than is necessary.

When your perfectly healthy baby wakes to feed or check in or get some comfort, it is normal. A lot of time, money and tears can be wasted trying to 'fix' your baby, who is indeed functioning at their best. Base your expectations on biology and you can avoid the pain of trying to force your baby to sleep. A baby will sleep for longer and longer stretches when they are ready to.

While a baby's biology has not changed in the past 40 years, our parenting practices certainly have. With fewer and fewer new parents having access to a village (or even grandparents), there are fewer arms available to rock babies and fewer chests to lie on for a nap. There is also less of a chance for mothers to learn spontaneously from those around them.

We are also well aware of the mental and physical health benefits of quality sleep. We want our babies, and ourselves, to have the best sleep possible. Naps help to lay down memory and contribute to learning, and a good night's sleep enhances your quality of life overall. We know sleep is important. And often we feel desperate to speed things up and help our baby's brain mature.

Is sleep training the magic pill?

Sleep training is a term used to describe a bunch of methods that hope to help babies sleep through the night. Sleep training methods vary considerably, from the old-fashioned 'cry it out' method (where babies are put in their cot and left until the next morning) to gentler sleep training methods such as 'camping out' (where parents sleep near but not with their baby) or 'delayed comforting' (where parents return to the crib to comfort their babies at set intervals, such as every three minutes).

Sleep training is also used in the literature to describe parental education about newborn sleep, as well as sleep hygiene practices. This makes it tricky to interpret sleep training research as it is difficult to isolate one method and say whether it works, or whether it works better than the others – and also for how long the effects are evident.

Most agree that sleep training is undesirable before a baby is four months old. Others say that parents must intervene before a baby is too old, at somewhere between four and six months. Others say to wait until your baby is no longer feeding at night – although for many babies this will be sometime in their second year of life. Older babies are thought to be more difficult to train as they are mobile and have the knowledge that their parents still exist even if they can't see them.

In my practice, I meet families who tell of amazing results thanks to sleep training, and others who have the opposite experience. It is important to note that 'for about 20% of babies, sleep training just doesn't work', as Jodi Mindell says. Yes, that's right. One out of every five babies will not sleep through the night, regardless of the method used.

'Your child may not be ready for sleep training, for whatever reason,' Mindell says. 'Maybe they're too young, or they're going through separation anxiety, or there may be an underlying medical issue, such as reflux.'

If we are going to parent smart and hard, the focus should be on helping your baby grow into a child who is a healthy sleeper – a lover of sleep and someone whose sleep integrates with your family's sleep culture. Try not to fixate on the exact times of naps or the number of times you are getting up at night. We are all different, and what is enough sleep for some may not be enough for you. Your baby may need more or less sleep than their peers. What healthy sleep looks like is going to vary for each family.

The question I ask families is, 'Is it working?' If the answer is yes, it is working for your family, don't try to change anything to reach any 'ideal'. There is no ideal. If the answer is no, it's not working, then we need to figure out why.

But how are you supposed to know if you and your baby are getting enough sleep? And what should you do if it is clear that something is not right? Let's answer some of the most common questions that new parents have about adequate sleep in the first year.

Defining adequate sleep

In my clinical practice, I work alongside two kinds of families:

1. Families whose babies clearly have disordered sleep, which is causing distress and dysfunction
2. The so-called worried well, whose babies are healthy and well and sleeping just as a baby should. These families have believed the sleep myths and are struggling to get their baby to do 'what the book says they should'.

Some babies may never, ever, sleep through the night as waking is literally programmed into their genes.

A twins study conducted at the Laval University in Quebec, Canada, has shed some interesting light on sleep genes. Dr Evelynne Touchette studied approximately 1 000 pairs of fraternal and identical twins. Fraternal twins share roughly 50 per cent of genes, while identical twins share closer to 100 per cent.

The study showed that genetics are the largest determinant for whether or not your child will sleep through the night. Parenting or the child's environment determines only a child's ability to take naps during the day. She was quick, however, to caution parents against giving up on practising good sleep hygiene. Sleep hygiene involves keeping a healthy bedroom environment and practising a good bedtime routine at about the same time each night.

'The genetic influence is only part of the equation that controls sleep duration. One should not give up on trying to correct inadequate sleep duration or bad sleep habits early in childhood,' reported Dr Touchette to LiveScience.

On the next page are the guidelines from the DST-NRF Centre of Excellence in Human Development that were released to the public in 2018:

What you can see is that, from birth to three months, your baby should sleep for a total of 14 to 17 hours per day. At about the four-month mark, once your baby has gained fat stores and started becoming more active in the day, they will sleep slightly less, for a total of 12 to 16 hours per day.

There is a big 'but' here. This total is accumulative. In the beginning, babies appear to cycle quickly between being awake and asleep. In fact, it is thought that newborn babies have hundreds of sleep/wake cycles, which is why many parents are uncertain about whether their baby is waking up or not. One moment they are stretching, the next they are totally relaxed and fast asleep.

BABIES
(BIRTH TO 1 YEAR)

MOVING **30** MINUTES

SITTING ✓ ✗ **0** HOURS

SLEEPING

0–3 MONTHS	4–11 MONTHS
14-17 HOURS	**12-16** HOURS

For babies, multiple wakings does not necessarily mean that there is a sleep problem. Their sleep cycles will gradually lengthen and become clearer.

If you are concerned, and planning to see a health professional, keep a two-week sleep diary and add their day naps to their night sleeps to get a sleep total.

Here are examples of adequate sleep with night wakings.

Example 1: A one-month-old who is feeding every 1.5 to 2.5 hours is likely to be sleeping for 45- to 60-minute stretches. Over a 24-hour period, this baby would be having 12 to 16 hours of sleep.

Example 2: A three-month-old baby who is having three day naps that are 90 minutes long each (day sleep = 4 hours 30 minutes) and then sleeps at night from 19:00 to 01:00 (sleep = 6 hours) and again from 02:00 to 3:30 (sleep = 1 hour 30 minutes) and from 04:00 to 06:30 (sleep = 2 hours 30 minutes). This would be a total of 14 hours and 45 minutes of sleep. This would be classed as adequate sleep.

Nap 1	90 minutes
Nap 2	90 minutes
Nap 3	90 minutes
Night 1	6 hours
Night 2	1 hour 30 minutes
Night 3	2 hours 45 minutes
Sleep total	*14 hours 45 minutes*

Example 3: A four-month-old who is having three day naps that are 45 minutes long (sleep = 2 hours 15 minutes) and sleep from 18:00 to 02:00 (sleep = 8 hours) and then from 03:00 to 05:00 (sleep = 2 hours). This would be a total of 12 hours 15 minutes sleep. This would be adequate sleep for this age.

Nap 1	45 minutes
Nap 2	45 minutes
Nap 3	45 minutes
Night 1	8 hours
Night 2	2 hours
Sleep total	*12 hours 15 minutes*

What becomes awfully clear is that adequate sleep for your baby may still mean that your sleep pattern is disrupted. You could be left sleep deprived even if your baby is getting adequate sleep.

What is probably more critical than counting the hours and minutes is paying attention to your behaviour and your baby's behaviour during the day.

How do I know if my baby is not getting enough sleep?

Truth be told, babies are pretty good at making sure they get all the sleep they need. However, there are some babies who experience sleep deprivation, usually due to health issues.

Here are some of the signs of how sleep-deprived young babies behave:

- A noted lack of interest in people and the environment
- A tendency to look away from stimulating things
- Hand-to-face gestures: pulling ears, rubbing eyes
- Fluttering eyelids
- Yawning.

Here are some of the signs of how sleep-deprived older babies behave:

- Becoming more accident-prone
- Becoming more 'clingy'
- Becoming ever-more active as the night wears on
- Struggling to deal with emotional upsets during the day, for example taking longer to get over something upsetting.

The signs of sleep deprivation in adults are not much different, except that adults rarely – if ever – become hyperactive. Most of us tend to end up becoming more hypoactive or lethargic.

You may be suffering from sleep deprivation if you have:

- Reduced cognitive skills – you are more easily distracted and forgetful than usual
- Emotional lability – you find yourself becoming very sad or very angry very quickly
- Avolition – you feel very demotivated and down
- Food cravings – you are relying on sweet, fatty foods and sweet, caffeinated drinks to get you through the day. Doughnut and coffee, anyone?

These symptoms would be relieved with sleep. You would feel 'like your old self' again after a good nap or good night. If these symptoms are not relieved by sleep, you could be experiencing postnatal depression. Talk to your partner about how you are feeling and seek the help of a health professional. Early diagnosis and intervention can limit the effects of this common postnatal illness.

What is normal in terms of napping?

A baby may spend up to 10 months in a dark womb. That is 40 weeks in the dark. This explains why newborn infants do not know day from night, and why they sleep in bits throughout the day and night. Between four and six weeks, as babies become more biologically stable, they may start sleeping for longer stretches at night and less during the day as their brains start to synch with the sun and secrete melatonin. This connection will only be complete at about three to four months of age. Babies will slowly drop day sleeps or naps as they grow older.

At six months, most babies need three daytime naps. At 12 months, most babies only need two naps. And at about 18 months, most children require only one daytime nap and are highly susceptible to parental influence for nighttime sleep duration. It is not clear why, but at this age sleep interventions are more successful than at any other age. It is hypothesised that there is significant brain maturation at this time.

Napping after two years of age is a cultural issue – in some homes, taking a nap or siesta is for the whole family. Other parents find that an afternoon nap upsets their toddler's ability to fall asleep and stay asleep at night. So, they dump it.

Your baby will usually nap for longer if you nap with them. Napping is a great way to top up your own sleep tank if you have a baby who wakes frequently at night. Nap with your baby or enjoy some alone time while they nap – whatever fills your tank the most.

What should I do if my baby falls asleep while feeding?

Humans are mammals – we suckle our young. If you watch mammals feed their babies (think pigs, rabbits, puppies, or kittens), you will notice that their babies fall asleep towards the end of the feed, usually on or near their mothers.

As if motherhood was not hard enough, along comes more bad parenting advice: 'Feed your baby when they wake and do not let them fall asleep while they are feeding – you will create a bad sleep association.'

And so moms are stroking heads and tickling backs and taking drowsy babies off the breast to wake them up before they put them in their cot to sleep. It's crazy, really, when you consider that:

- Drinking milk makes babies sleepy. When a baby nurses, their body responds by releasing hormones such as oxytocin, which causes sleepiness.
- Breast milk changes in composition towards the end of the day to further support falling asleep during evening and night feeds. Why would you not use this to your advantage?

By interrupting feeds to try to foster an 'independent' sleeper, you may actually cause feeding problems. A baby who knows that a feed could end before they are full may become anxious and unable to relax while feeding. The body needs to rest to digest, but a baby whose body is full of cortisol will not be able to do this – and, of course, will not be able to fall asleep due to fear.

This is a great time to talk about non-nutritive sucking (NNS) . . . NNS, or sucking to soothe and/or to fall asleep, is why some babies love to suck their fingers/your fingers/a dummy/a blanket. They may not be hungry; sucking just feels good. If your baby is sucking their thumb or a dummy to fall asleep, you do not have a 'self-soother' – you have a baby who likes to suck to fall asleep.

If you have a baby who only wants the real deal and refuses to use anything other than you for non-nutritive sucking, it will be tougher for you than it is for parents whose babies are happy to suck their own thumb or dummy. This *sucks* (sorry, but the pun was just waiting to be exploited!) – but more for you than for your baby. The bad news is that you will have to be around when your baby wants to suck to fall asleep. The good news is that your baby trusts you and thinks that you are their happy place.

Other good news is that some babies will choose not to suck to sleep, but will prefer to be comforted by other non-nutritive things:

- Some babies will love being swaddled or held tightly.
- Others will enjoy hearing a specific song as they drift off.
- Some babies love to be rocked – there is a reason why rocking chairs have stayed popular over centuries.
- Others may enjoy holding a comforting toy or blanket, usually one that has been with them through the good, the bad and the ugly. Lose it at your peril!

Again, forcing your baby to suck a dummy is not going to work. Your baby will show you their preferred way of being comforted and falling asleep, and you will do well to use it to your advantage. By all means, try a dummy for a few weeks – but if your baby does not want it, ditch it.

Nobody walks down the aisle with a dummy in their mouth, right? But how much dummy is enough? And how much is too much? Here are some guidelines for dummy use:

- Once you find the type of dummy that your baby loves, stock up on it. Keep it in a few special locations – one in your baby bag, one in your pram and one close to where your baby sleeps.

- Sterilise dummies regularly until your baby has started solids. To sterilise dummies, follow the same process as you do to sterilise bottles. This helps to kill and prevent oral thrush, a common yeast-like fungal infection that affects young babies and can spread to their mothers. Thrush needs to be treated from mouth to anus, so ask your doctor to help should you suspect thrush.

- Once your baby has started solids and is mouthing many, many objects anyway, you only have to wash the dummy with soap and hot water. It will be impossible to keep all objects that enter their mouth sterile. In fact, you do not want to. It's time to let your baby face some germs and develop a solid immune system.

- Babies should only be given their dummies when they need them. This could be when they are uncomfortable or when they are sleepy.

- Avoid using dummy chains for naps and at night, as they can be hazardous. The dummy will usually fall out once your baby falls into a deep sleep and stops sucking. If you want to make it easier for your baby to find the dummy when they wake, remove the dummy from your baby's mouth and place it in its designated 'sleep spot'. You can show your baby where the dummy lives at night so that they can reach out for it as needed as they get older. Most babies will understand this from about nine months old.

- Ask your baby to put the dummy in its 'sleep spot' when it is time to sing or play. Under a pillow is usually helpful. Your baby should have more dummy-free time than dummy time. It is important when they are calm and alert to practise babbling and cooing, rather than only practising sucking. An older baby should be encouraged to remove the dummy when they speak and not to speak around the dummy.

- For older children, you can set dummy boundaries if you start to notice that it is getting in the way of normal development. For example, they can choose to leave their dummy in their school bag if they attend day care or in the dashboard of your car if they feel it will be safer there.

- Your baby may be using a dummy too much if it starts to change the shape of their jaw or their teeth. However, there are many other things that can cause these changes, such as mouth breathing and lack of chewing solid foods.

- Getting rid of a dummy can be a breeze (if a child is ready to move on) or a great challenge (if the child is not ready). It is probably too soon to get rid of a dummy if your child is traumatised, rather than excited, when you bring up the idea of giving their dummy to a small baby or the Easter bunny or the dummy fairy. Your baby may use a dummy for far longer than you expected – and that's okay.

And what do you do if your baby is sucking their thumb? Unlike a dummy, you cannot take your baby's thumbs away. If your baby loves sucking their thumb, remember that they have loved doing this since they were in your womb. It is an engrained pattern.

The upside? You can enjoy the fact that your baby will never lose their dummy. The downside? You won't be able to change this habit for a few years. Some families have tried to discourage thumb sucking by painting their baby's thumb with hot sauce. In my experience, I have only seen this cause fury in the short term, with no long term success. Truly, there is nothing you can do about a thumb sucker. Besides, they won't suck their thumb forever.

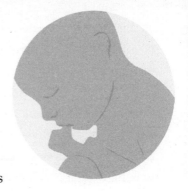

What is a good bedtime routine?

A bedtime routine refers to the activities that lead up to bedtime. A routine is a sequence of actions followed regularly. It is often advised that you practise the same bedtime routine religiously to create an expectation of bedtime in the brain. A good routine is largely a predictable one.

Each family will have its own sequence of events due to its own family rhythm. Some families prefer bathing their babies in the morning, rather than at night. Others believe that their babies sleep better after a warm bath. Others, still, will say that bath time makes their baby too excited and hyped up to sleep. What is more important than what you do is the order in which you do it.

If you decide to do supper, bath, bottle and bedtime story, you will need to try to keep this going. If your baby starts going to bed at roughly the same time each night and waking at roughly the same time each morning, they have established a circadian rhythm and you can celebrate that predicting their sleep will be easier.

Choosing to put your child down with the sun can also help,

as this is when the sleep hormone melatonin is produced. Harnessing the sun's superpower will be easier for families who live in regions where the sun sets at about bedtime.

While most researchers have looked at what happens in the hour before bedtime, I have seen – at the practice, as well as in my own children's lives – that the day's events also affect bedtime. Babies who have not seen their parents all day may need more time to reconnect before bedtime. These babies may need a later bedtime. Babies who live in a busy household may need to go to bed earlier, as their days are so full of interaction. The ideal routine is the one that works for your family.

What is sleep hygiene?

So, your baby did not hit the sleep gene jackpot. There's not much you can do about that, then. But there are many things you can do to make falling asleep and staying asleep more likely in the future. It's also nice to know that you've ticked all the boxes when the sleep questions get hurled your way.

Sleep hygiene is about habits and practices that relate to good sleep. This means including certain things to support a good night's sleep (healthy supper, warm bath, brushing teeth, calming bedtime stories and into bed) and excluding certain sleep baddies such as fabrics that are rough or have a strong or bad smell (consider your bed linen and you and your baby's pyjamas), sugar and caffeine (for you if you are breastfeeding, and for baby if they are on solids), as well as any screen time exposure for baby (TV, computer, iPad etc.).

If you have a baby who can fall asleep in front of the TV, aren't you lucky. For most babies, it is helpful to fall asleep in a quiet, dark room that is about 21 degrees Celsius. Many parents have

been saved by installing block-out curtains (to block out the light) and switching on a fan (to block out the household noises and prevent mosquitoes from chomping on your precious baby).

Issues that interfere with sleep

You may notice that something is interfering with your baby's sleep. Your baby is tired, but struggles to fall asleep or possibly struggles to stay asleep. While sleep disorders are fairly rare, there are many health issues that are common sleep thieves. I define sleep thieves as the most common issues that rob children of sleep. These are reflux disease, colic, allergic rhinitis, eczema, ear infections and teething pain.

Some sleep thieves come in the early days; others may appear only after a few weeks or months. If you notice a sudden change in your baby's sleep pattern, a check-up at your paediatrician (preferably one who has a special interest in sleep) will be well worth it to determine the underlying cause.

Here is how each of these sleep thieves typically present, to help you work out whether there could be more to your baby's waking.

Reflux versus gastro-oesophageal reflux disease (GORD)

There is a difference between vomiting and reflux disease. Most babies have an immature valve at the top of their stomachs, allowing some milk (and sometimes acid) to run back into the throat. This can happen when the baby lies down, or even when the stomach pressure is increased by straining or with normal digestive movements. Therefore, most babies posset after a feed – this is nothing to worry about. A little bit of milk may be pushed out with an air bubble when winding your baby after a feed. This is normal, and not GORD. If your baby is happy and thriving, and not overly distressed by the vomits, you do not need to worry.

Sometimes, however, excessive stomach acid escapes into the oesophagus. If it stays in contact with the wall of the oesophagus for extended periods, it can burn the baby's oesophagus. This is very painful, and can cause serious damage to the oesophagus and prevent a baby from taking in enough milk to grow. It can also cause a baby to start refusing feeds when awake, drinking more at night while half-asleep and desperately hungry. Some babies may start to refuse feeds altogether as swallowing is so painful.

This is known as GORD. It requires treatment to limit damage and help a baby get the nourishment they need. It is more common in premature babies and babies with low muscle tone. Muscle tone is the readiness of muscle fibres to contract when at rest (see page 31 for a more detailed explanation).

Babies with GORD will often fall asleep after a feed, but as soon as they are placed lying down on their backs, they will wake with a startle and loud cry (wail!). There may be no vomiting (silent reflux) or an impressive vom-bomb that drenches them and their cot. When they lie on their backs, they may arch their back and look over their right shoulder. They will also cry a lot after feeds. This is all in response to the burning-acid feeling in their throats and tummies. Reflux can and should be treated to prevent an inflamed oesophagus.

According to paediatrician and allergologist Dr Claudia Gray, manifestations of pathological reflux that require medical attention are as follows:

1. Extreme irritability, discomfort after feeds and feed refusal
2. Excessive loss of calories, leading to poor growth
3. Recurrent chestiness because of aspiration (breathing in) of stomach contents.

Visit your paediatrician if you suspect reflux disorder. Milder cases may respond to prolonged upright positioning after feeds or frequent smaller feeds. More severe cases may need medication to reduce stomach acidity and reduce the 'burning' of the refluxed material. Antacids are not without complications: they can lead to an increased susceptibility to infections, because you are knocking out stomach acid – which is the first line of defence against many infections. They can also lead to a disrupted microbiome (natural bugs living in harmony) in the gut, and to constipation. However, in some cases the benefits of the antacids outweigh the risks, and they can lead to significant relief of pain, increased feeding and reduced irritability. In very severe cases, surgery may be required.

Colic

Colic is a term to describe an otherwise healthy baby who fusses and cries for a few consecutive hours each day. The crying often peaks in the evenings between 17:00 and 20:00 – although it could happen at any predictable time of the day.

The phenomenon of colic is not entirely understood. Some say it is a symptom of overstimulation and a sign of immature brain development. Another theory is that it is a digestive problem, possibly brought on by a build-up of lactose (the sugar found in milk) that can be difficult for small babies to digest. This partially digested milk upsets the colon, causing it to contract and cramp. Babies who struggle with colic typically pull up their legs and clench their fists.

Parents of babies with colic may have a tough time getting their baby to sleep at night, although they usually sleep well once they have fallen asleep. The good news is that colic usually disappears as suddenly as it came, at about three to four months of age. While you wait for that to happen, you can try the following strategies:

- Encourage sucking a dummy, which promotes gut motility.
- Place a warm pack on your baby's tummy when you see or hear signs of cramping.
- Practise baby wearing by using a baby sling or blanket, and keep your baby close to your body to help soothe the pain.
- Playing white noise may help soothe your baby. Many believe this noise mimics the sounds your baby would have

become accustomed to in your belly. Not sure what white noise is? Think the dull, constant sound of a hairdryer, vacuum cleaner or fan. The good news is that you can easily download white noise to play for your baby, instead of leaving an appliance running.

- There are many colic remedies, but be sure the ingredients are safe and listed on the container.

Allergic rhinitis or nasal blockage

Babies have small noses that easily become blocked. A simple cold in a baby can lead to significant sleep disruption.

Sometimes allergies lead to itchy and irritable mucous membranes. This is more common in toddlers and children, but can occur early on in some babies. The inner eyes, nose, sinuses and throat can become itchy and inflamed. Babies appear tired but struggle to fall asleep. They rub their nose a lot when awake and when asleep. They seem irritable. Inside their nose it is very congested, so they mouth breathe and may even snore as loudly as an obese man! They struggle to reach deep sleep and usually wake between sleep cycles.

These babies are tired because the congestion prevents them from moving from light sleep to deep sleep. They are frustrated, as they really want to sleep. An oral antihistamine and nose spray are usually prescribed by a doctor. Allergy testing can be done to determine what your baby is allergic to, so that you can limit contact with allergens as far as possible. Although grass, tree pollen and household dust are very hard to avoid altogether, you could limit your exposure and hopefully improve your baby's sleep.

Parents of babies who have allergies recommend the following:

- Keeping pets out of the bedroom

- Removing carpets where possible
- Decluttering to avoid dust gathering
- Regularly washing bedding, mattresses and pillows
- Regularly using a damp cloth and vacuum to clean all surfaces
- Using a saline solution to wash the allergens out of the baby's nose every evening before applying nasal spray.

If the allergic rhinitis results in enlarged adenoids and tonsils, these may have to be removed to allow the baby to breathe without obstructions.

Eczema

The itch of eczema is what disturbs babies, preventing them from falling asleep and staying asleep. You may see them scratching at their creases (armpits, elbows, wrists and knees) while in a light sleep, or you could see scratch marks when you change them in the morning. Their skin seems to be itchier at night than during the day, as this is when histamine levels rise.

Protecting their sleep starts with protecting their skin. A visit to your doctor will yield help – through learning what to avoid (certain foods and chemicals) and what to do (using emollients to create a fatty barrier over the skin to limit dehydration and irritation). Many babies outgrow eczema as children, but it needs to be treated to avoid discomfort and skin infections in the short term and attention difficulties in the longer term.

Earache

Babies are born with very narrow inner-ear tubes, which makes it easy for infections to brew and difficult for babies to equalise the pressure in their ears when there is a change in air pressure (such as on an aeroplane). Both swimmer's ear (when water is lodged in the inner ear from the pool, sea, or bath) and a middle-ear infection (when bacteria-filled fluid creates an infection and pressure in the middle ear) may be excruciatingly painful, especially once the baby lies down to sleep.

The earache cry is often very loud and distressing, and babies will usually hold and pull violently at their ear or the side of their head or jaw. It is relieved by treating the pressure and pain with eardrops prescribed by your nurse or doctor and, when necessary, an oral antibiotic. It can be confused with teething pain, as this also causes babies to pull at their ears. Babies with recurrent middle-ear infections will need grommets to protect their hearing. A grommet is a tube that helps to keep the ear canal open and allows fluid to drain from the ear. A baby may need only one grommet, or one for each ear.

Teething pain

Babies cut 20 teeth somewhere between birth and the age of 36 months. Some babies seem undisturbed by this; others show symptoms of profound discomfort. Many parents report that when their baby is cutting a tooth they have a raised temperature, skin rashes, green, runny, or foul-smelling stools, loss of appetite and difficulty sleeping.

Similar symptoms may occur due to viral infections picked up by contact with other sick people – and especially during all the mouthing that babies do to soothe their gums. Viruses and teething are not always easy to distinguish from each other.

Dentists advise addressing the teething pain during the day and at night to break the pain cycle. What's more difficult to address is when to start or stop medicating – at times it will feel like your baby has been teething for months! Treating the teething pain with a combination of paracetamol and ibuprofen should bring relief. Ask your pharmacist or paediatrician for the right dose of each according to your baby's weight and age.

Here are guidelines I use for when medication is suitable for teething pain:

- Your baby refuses to drink or eat during the day.
- Your baby is obviously tired, but cannot sleep due to the pain.
- Topical treatments are not, well, *cutting* it (teething powder, numbing solutions, ice chewies, etc.).
- You can feel and/or see a tooth underneath the hot, red gum, and it is quite clear that it is cutting through the gum. There may even be bleeding.

Apart from medications, other soothing strategies include using touch and non-nutritive sucking to try to help your baby cope better with teething pain. Holding your baby close to you and offering them a chance to suck your breast or their dummy can help them subjectively experience less pain.

I can feel your anxiety building as you start to consider the thought of giving your precious, untouched, drug-free baby medication. I know how difficult it is to accept that your baby may have a problem that requires you to give them over-the-counter or prescription drugs. It took me a long time to accept that both my babies had reflux that required chronic, daily medication (okay, so it was slightly easier the second time around!).

I was worried about the side effects and concerned about the long-term impact. I had promised myself that for the first six months all my babies would ingest would be my pure breast milk to ensure a healthy gut. I didn't want them to have preservatives or sugar, let alone schedule 5 drugs. I weaned my first baby off her reflux medication many times in the first four months to check whether she could live without it. I was faced with this truth: she needed this medicine and I needed to give it to her, despite what I had planned before meeting her. The benefits outweighed the risks.

I encounter the same resistance regarding giving medicine to a baby when I speak to other parents at my practice. Parents are anxious about giving their baby anything, even after a doctor has made a diagnosis and prescribed a drug. Babies are so small and so precious and drugs are so toxic and so scary. Yes, that can be true.

But pain is pain, whether you are big or small. And pain needs to be addressed. If a condition is left untreated, it does not magically disappear – it usually worsens and becomes harder to treat later. Help your baby. If a doctor has prescribed medication, trial it. Watch and see how it affects your baby's symptoms. Remember, no medicine has to be taken forever. You are not taking the easy way out. You are giving your baby the pain control they need.

Pain control for babies has improved greatly in hospitals as health professionals have learnt to recognise and respect a baby's pain cues. You would do well to do the same, because we know that pain that is not treated may be remembered and could cause many aversions and issues further down the parenting road.

Why haven't scientists found the magic formula to get my baby to sleep through the night?

There is no magic formula because this is not a one-size-fits-all journey. No two parenting journeys will be the same. You can learn from others, but you need to make your own choices and live with the consequences.

Again, apply the 'Is it working?' philosophy. If you return home after a busy day and want to feed your baby to sleep, go for it. If you like co-sleeping, practise this safely without guilt. If you need more space from your baby to sleep well, camp out or use a baby monitor so you feel less anxious about leaving them alone. Do what works for your family as a whole. You have a long road ahead of you.

Parenting is hard. It involves sacrificing. So, when there is a moment of pure bliss, soak it up. For me, this has included catching a glimpse of my baby's top lip all pert and full after a marathon feeding session; watching my babies' lips suck long after the bottle or dummy has been removed; hearing my toddlers sing the songs I sang to them as babies (that I had forgotten all about); and taking in their smell each evening after they have put on their pyjamas.

Harness the power of oxytocin to maintain a close bond with your baby both before and after they start sleeping through the night. It will help you and baby to feel closer and calmer.

On the other hand, expecting that your baby will not wake at night could be setting yourself up for failure. If you think your baby should not be waking, and they do wake, you are going to have a big emotional response. When this happens, your body will fill with adrenaline and cortisol as you wake. If you breastfeed your baby at this point, these stress hormones can pass through your milk to your baby and make it more difficult for both of you to fall asleep again. Lowering your expectations may help to increase the amount of sleep you get at night as you don't waste time stewing about the fact that you have had to get up to see to your baby.

Let's recap what you can control regarding your baby's sleep:

- Where they sleep – which room, the temperature of the room, the amount of light in the room
- Whom they sleep with
- What time the family rises in the morning
- Whether they sleep with or without you
- What your baby sleeps in – you choose the linen, pyjamas, layers etc.
- The bedtime routine the hour before bed.

And let's recap what you can't control:

- When they fall sleep – you can't force anyone to fall asleep
- When they wake up – your baby's sleep genes play the biggest part in their nighttime waking
- Your baby's age and stage, or neurological maturity – younger babies need regular care and feeding
- Interrupted sleep due to occasional illnesses and teething
- Interrupted sleep due to dreams and/or nightmares
- Your baby practising skills unconsciously while asleep – sleep tends to regress as they learn a new skill
- Your baby's anxiety levels, especially regarding separation anxiety
- Health issues such as reflux and colic.

Unathi's story

Unathi was born to a teenage mother. Shortly after her birth, she was diagnosed with oesophageal atresia – when the oesophagus does not connect properly to the stomach. A baby with this condition can swallow milk, but it does not flow down into the tummy as there is a blockage. This blockage forms early on in the pregnancy, but only becomes a problem once the baby is born and needs to drink and eat orally rather than receive nutrition from the umbilical cord.

Unathi underwent surgery to join her oesophagus and her stomach together. The surgery could give her a connection, but as her wounds would need time to heal she would need to be fed via a PEG (a tube that goes directly into the small intestine to bypass the oesophagus and stomach). It would give her nutrition while she healed and grew stronger.

For her young mother – who had not planned to have a baby, let alone a baby who needed multiple surgeries and hospitalisation – this was all too much. She left the hospital and did not return.

Unathi experienced immense physical pain, as well as immense psychological pain. She needed to be upright and still, so she remained strapped in a car seat in a hospital bed while her digestive system healed and matured. The nursing staff interacted regularly with her, but she did not have a dedicated caregiver with whom she had bonded. She would fall asleep in this position by rocking her head from side to side with her eyes closed.

When she was nine months old, I started working with her with the aim of providing developmental stimulation. She was understandably very behind her peers. What became clear was that, although she was no longer in pain, she had a clear memory of the pain she had experienced. The memory of the pain was as distressing as the pain itself. She could not separate the two. She was fearful of being on her back (as she had experienced reflux in this position) and she was fearful of being on her tummy (as she had two large, red, hypersensitive scars from her surgeries). She was also fearful of being carried, as she had become used to staying in one place.

I had to work slowly and respectfully to make progress. The first step was to limit pain by ensuring that the reflux medication was given regularly to avoid any oesophageal pain and that there were no further painful procedures performed without pain control. The second step was to show her that touch and movement could be pleasant rather than painful.

The first breakthrough came when she was happy to lie on my chest and push up through her arms to look at my face. Over the next few months, she started to roll and explore moving in and out of sitting. She was pulling to stand and cruising around the ward much to the delight of the staff. What was more difficult to target was her fear of food. She did not know what food was, how you ate it or why you would even want to do this. The memory of pain on swallowing seemed to remain, despite her blockage having been clear for months.

It was only through a multidisciplinary approach to feeding therapy under the care of a stoma sister, dietitian, speech therapist and occupational therapist that Unathi started to play and explore foods. Progress was slow, but eventually she had her PEG removed and was able to return home under her grandmother's care.

She continued to use head rocking from side to side to go to sleep. Even though she was now able to run and climb and roll around and shared a bed with her granny, this remained her preferred way of going to sleep. Once a pattern is entrenched, it is hard to change. But not all patterns can or need to be changed. For Unathi, rocking her head from side to side did not cause her or her family any distress or dysfunction. It would be a 'habit of childhood' that she would outgrow.

Jedd's story

Jedd was a pretty good sleeper. When he was a newborn, he took to swaddling and loved his dummy and doo-doo toy. He was not easily startled by his pet dogs barking or his parents' household activities. He woke up reliably once a night for a feed, and later could be put back to sleep pretty quickly if you popped his dummy back in his mouth.

He was an early walker, at nine months. Along with more mobility and freedom came separation anxiety. Suddenly he needed to be held to fall asleep, at nap time and at night. He no longer wanted just his dummy and doo-doo if he woke at night: he wanted to be picked up and held by his mom or dad.

By the time he turned one, his parents were tired. This new clinginess was exhausting, and they longed for the days when the dummy used to work its magic. His parents were both back at their full-time jobs and resenting the 30 to 60 minutes it took to get him down with each waking. After looking for a better way, they found a popular parenting book and decided to give sleep training a go. After all, he had been such a good sleeper. Surely they could get him back to that?

Jedd's parents had always been high achievers, and they wanted to get this thing right – first time. They followed the sleep training programme step by step. This meant leaving him to cry for increasing intervals until he fell asleep. After three nights of intense 'protesting', Jedd had not taught himself to sleep through the night. He had, however, taught himself to climb out of his cot.

He also refused to be put into his cot – at all. By anybody.

It was at this point that his parents made contact with me, as suddenly they had a worse problem on their hands: a one-year-old who was no longer safe to be left in his cot.

The question was, 'At how old, and when, should you move a baby to a bed? We officially have a climber.'

As I dug to find out what had sparked the climbing, I got this message from his mom: 'I think it is because we sleep trained him (well, tried) he's basically petrified of the cot. It's so traumatic! Takes us over an hour to get him to nap now in the day and he screams blue murder even if he is in your arms because he thinks you are going to put him in his cot. He has bruised his chest from trying to escape! But the sleep doctor said we must just do it for a few days and he will adjust . . . We don't feel comfortable closing his door now. What if he gets hurt as he climbs out his cot?'

The solution I suggested was to ditch sleep training and rebuild trust. They could use his existing understanding of language and say 'bye-bye' to his cot. A double mattress was then to be bought into the room and put on the floor to allow Jedd and one or both of his parents to fit next to him.

It would take time to make him feel safe again. His door was to be left open, as well as his parents' bedroom door, but all other doors in the house were to be closed for safety reasons. It was essential that Jedd felt he had access to his parents should he need it.

His dad was not so keen on the mattress-on-the-floor idea, so he built a gorgeous wooden 'house' structure that matched their Scandinavian home décor style. Jedd responded beautifully to his new 'big boy' bed and his parents reported that his best time of the day was stories with Dad.

I do not know where his parents are sleeping today. They may be playing musical beds every night – but to be honest, as long as there is more shared joy and less shared anxiety, I am happy with the outcome.

My story:
The Tuesday-night sleepover

My first-born, Sophie, had terrible reflux. At her six-week check-up she vomited so badly in the waiting room that by the time I entered the doctor's office I was being handed a script for a more meaningful dose of antacid meds rather forcefully. I'd had strong ideas about not using any meds at all and keeping my child's gut sealed for the first year, so with hindsight I am glad that the doctor made it clear that this was essential and not optional.

On these meds, her burnt oesophagus began to heal and she could drink small volumes frequently. The tablets did not stop her vom-bombing, as we called it (it was rather spectacular), but they did take away the pain she had experienced when, at the end of each feed, acid had rushed back up her throat. We could help minimise the amount that she did vomit by holding her upright after she had fed, and also while she slept.

We did this in two ways – firstly, using a serious wedge that helped her lie uphill (head higher than feet) in her cot. And secondly, by lying her on her tummy and placing her on our chests when we sat upright on a couch.

As she grew older, the wedge proved less effective as she started rolling downhill. She was like a bucket; we needed to keep her food from pouring out. If she found herself flat at the bottom of the hill, out came the food. She needed to keep the food in so she could grow while her tummy sphincter matured and her trunk got stronger.

By the time she was a few months old, I was so sleep deprived that I started to experience sleep hallucinations – the most scary times when you are half-awake, half-asleep, and not sure whether you are dreaming or awake. The one night I lost her and was so distressed that I woke my husband – only for him to point out that she was in my arms.

At the six-month visit, when I asked, 'When can we stop the meds?', the paediatrician had bluntly told me that 'you walk away from reflux': the reflux would no longer need to be treated once she was walking. We clearly had a few more rough months ahead of us, so I volunteered to try sleeping out once a week.

To get a full eight hours sleep I would stay at my great friend, Anna Venter's, house. My husband would handle the night feeds with a bottle. I would pull in after putting Sophie to sleep at about 8 p.m. and set my alarm for 5 a.m. – to be home to do a morning feed. Wednesdays, the day after my epic eight-hour sleep, were magical days; I had so much more patience and capacity.

Looking back, I strongly advise all parents who have children with medical problems that interrupt sleep to take shifts. It is unhelpful to have two parents awake at the same time. In an ideal world I would plan to do two nights on and two nights off, so that you and your partner can find some solid sleep regularly. And if sleeping out is the only way to do it, I recommend giving it a try.

My story: Hard is not wrong

When my first baby was four and a half months old, we moved out of our teeny flat into a three-bedroom townhouse. Hindsight: moving with a teeny reflux baby is not a good idea! After a month of trying to look after her and set up a new home, I called in a visit from our pastor's wife. She had two lovely little girls and looked like she just loved being a mom. I thought she seemed like a good person to ask what I could do better.

She asked me how it was going and what I said was something like, 'Everything's fine as long as I'm holding her. If I try to do anything, we both fall apart.' By 'do anything', I meant putting her down so I could do things that I needed and wanted to do, especially after the move. I wanted her recommendations about some piece of equipment or routine that would allow me to set up home and feel more in control. She asked me, 'What would this piece of equipment be like?'

'Well, it would need to keep her upright because of the reflux, and warm and maybe move very gently and sing a little when her tummy is cramping . . .'

She started laughing and said, 'It sounds like what you are describing is a mother's arms.' Man, I was shattered. It suddenly hit me that my world was not going to be mended by buying a bouncy chair. I was not going to get out of this that easily. This was going to be my new normal for a while.

And then she said, 'Just because what you are doing is hard, doesn't mean that what you are doing is wrong.'

Alas, I had bought the lies that the books were selling. You know, the lies we would love to believe: that if you follow step 1, 2 and 3, or buy products A, B and C, motherhood will be easy, breezy, magazine-cover peasy. The lie that, if you are finding life hard, you can't be doing it right.

The truth is that it won't be easy. Life is difficult and messy without children. Parenthood is a whole new level of difficult and messy.

Useful advice from those who have gone before you

Sleep when baby sleeps

It is tempting to squeeze in some work/chores/social media scrolling when your baby is sleeping, but do not be fooled. The best gift you can give yourself and your family is to rest and reset. You may hate napping in the day. Well, get over it! You will need to make up the hours you lose at night. Pick a nap and commit to staying on your back until baby wakes. Resting is a great way to give your body some love, and it can increase milk supply.

Let the laundry and dishes wait

You may have to lower your expectations when it comes to housekeeping. Your baby will need you more than you may have imagined, leaving less time for you to keep your home as you like it. If you employ a housekeeper, this will be less of an issue for you, but if you are trying to juggle caring for your baby and cleaning the house, pick the baby over the house more often than the other way around.

Ask for help

You'll be surprised at how often you may need to ask for help. At best, this can be humbling; at worst, it's just plain annoying. But in asking for help you will be lucky enough to find your tribe: the crew that will go above and beyond to help you keep it together. And don't worry – you will have many chances to return the favour. Find friends who love you and your baby, and who offer a soft place to land. The African proverb that it takes a village to raise a child is true for all moms.

Take care of yourself

Most parents tend to shift their focus off themselves and on to their baby. This is essential for baby to survive. However, staying in this mode for too long can be devastating both for your health and your family's. Moms are the engine of the family, so you owe it to everyone to keep your engine running smoothly. You need to sleep. You need to eat. And you need to do things you love, whether that's going for a walk, baking or surfing. Whatever it is, try to carve out some time to refill your soul. You might not be able to do this every day, but as the saying goes, you can't draw water from an empty well. Find what works for you and your partner, and encourage each other to look after yourselves.

Accept that babies are different

I have touched on this many times already but it's so important that I'm going to say it again. Accepting your new life with your baby is half the battle won. Trying to change the way your baby sleeps or feeds to meet somebody else's expectations is exhausting. Try your best to be present and enjoy the season. The days are long, but the years are short.

REALITY 6: There is no magic formula that will make your baby sleep through the night

- One in every five babies is never going to sleep through the night, no matter what you do.
- The Unicorn Baby falls asleep alone in their cot. They do not need to be fed or held or rocked to sleep. They sleep all night through. Your baby may not do this. And that's okay.
- Night wakings are a biological norm. Healthy babies wake at night. If your baby's waking is causing you or your baby distress, visit your doctor to rule out any medical reason for waking.
- Babies love sucking to fall asleep. Do not rob your baby of this pleasure. It is a wonderful thing to see your baby drifting off to sleep at the end of a feed.

178

- Do what works for your family to get as much sleep as possible. Naps can help – so can practising a good bedtime routine and sleep hygiene.
- You can't force a baby to sleep. You also can't force a sleepy baby to feed.
- Don't be afraid to ask for help.
- Hard is not wrong.

Healthy babies wake at night

Signs that you are busting Myth 6

✔ Your baby likes sleeping (even if you think they should sleep for longer!).

✔ You have found a bedtime routine that works for your family.

✔ You expect your baby to wake at night, so you don't have a big emotional response when this happens. Your body is not filling with adrenaline and cortisol with each feed.

✔ You have discovered the power of napping (for you and for baby).

✔ You have found a sleep plan that works for your family. (PS: Playing musical beds is an acceptable sleep plan.)

Myth 7
Your baby grows and develops every day

The Unicorn Baby's growth and development is as predictable as their feeds and naps. They have gained the same amount of weight each week at their wellness visits, and fit perfectly into the clothing that is made for their age. They are consistently just above the growth curve. Their behaviour is predictable – at night and during the day. They do not have days when they are more or less hungry, or more or less happy. They are just moving slowly along the curve as they should.

The day you leave the hospital, you receive your baby's 'Road to Health' or vaccination chart. Usually, in this booklet, there will be a growth chart and a developmental chart. Your baby's birth weight, length and head circumference are recorded by a nursing sister in this book usually right after the birth, and then again upon discharge from the hospital. At each clinic visit, the nurse updates these charts to check that your baby is growing and developing well.

Growth charts are based on the growth of a sample of children from a particular place. Their growth is often measured at set points such as one, two, four, six and eight weeks of age, followed by measurements monthly until one year of age. Thereafter, measurements may be taken every six months. From the data that is gathered at these points in time, a growth curve will be created.

The most widely used growth chart from 1979 onwards was produced in the USA by the National Center for Health Statistics (NCHS). Many felt this measure was biased. Firstly, it was only representative of American babies and secondly, it was based on babies who were fed using formula.

So, in 1993 the World Health Organization commissioned an investigation and found that the NCHS curves were not suitable indicators for growth of all children, and that new curves were required. From 1997 to 2003, another study was held in six countries with different social and economic conditions to create the new WHO standards. In the new WHO standards, a baby who is growing up on breastmilk, rather than formula, was presented as the normal growth pattern. This was an important step towards making the charts a more reliable way to tell whether a child was suffering from malnutrition.

This new curve helps parents and health professionals monitor whether a baby is growing well. The growth charts are especially helpful in detecting when a baby is falling off their curve. This means they are not growing enough and may need more help to keep growing. However, by joining the growth points together to form a curve, the standards give the impression that children grow every day.

Back in 1981, in Pennsylvania in the USA, an anthropologist, Michelle Lampl, started researching growth. She was interested in a baby's head circumference, length and weight. She started by measuring babies weekly and noticed, 'Hey, babies grow weekly.' Then she had an interesting thought: 'Do they really take the whole week to grow this much?' So, she started measuring the babies twice weekly. Again, she thought: 'Does it really take a half a week for these babies to grow? Are these babies growing slowly and continuously through time?' And so she started measuring the babies daily.

What she discovered was that babies did not grow every day. Growth happened in jumps, or spurts. A baby would have a period of no growth, which she called stasis, followed by a period of sudden growth, which she called saltation. In a single 24-hour period, babies could grow by 0.5–1.65 cm in one day. The frequency of growth ranged from one event every 2 days to one event every 28 days.

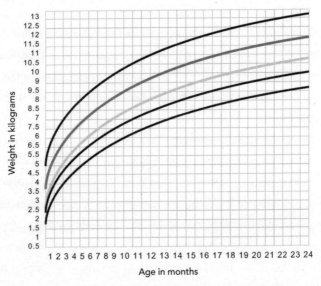

Percentile growth curves. Note that this graph is only by way of illustration and should not be used to track your baby's growth.

What she also noted is that a baby's behaviour would change during these periods of growth. They were often hungrier and had more tantrums, and there were changes in their sleeping patterns. This was a big discovery. At the time, it was assumed that all babies grew slowly and steadily, that the growth should go unnoticed. Similarly, a baby's metabolic needs and behaviour were seen as stable – feeding times and volume were set by age alone.

What this discovery confirmed is that i) a baby's needs fluctuate from day to day and ii) growing changes behaviour. If we are to accept that it is common for babies to have growth spurts, we will have to accept that it is necessary for babies to go 'off script' and feed more or less as needed.

What I find remarkable is how what we know now empirically about a baby's growth matches what mothers have known for years. For example, we know that the first two months of a baby's life is the greatest period of growth in the first year. Isn't it wonderful, then, that your small baby, in their first eight weeks of life, feeds so frequently? Yes – initially, your baby is feeding to build up your supply of breast milk. Thereafter, however, they are feeding so that they can grow exponentially. There is a beautiful partnership between mother and baby.

Unfortunately, parents are tempted to focus solely on the numbers. Some mothers may be so anxious about ensuring that their baby is growing well that they choose to weigh their baby after every feed. This is a sure-fire way to know that your baby is taking in milk (breastfeeding can feel mysterious to many who can't tell how much their baby is getting). But what it doesn't tell you is whether your baby has taken in enough – only your baby can tell you that.

What does weighing a baby tell us?

Weighing a baby on a regular scale will only tell you the mass gained. The scale cannot tell you where the growth has occurred. Was it the brain? Or did it become body fat? Was it used to grow strong bones? Or did it become muscle? While we want growth to happen in all these places, the current literature tells us that a gain in muscle mass is the best kind of growth to watch for as it is this growth that is the predictor for healthy development. Your body will only grow muscle mass after all the other essential organs have had what they need. So, muscle mass means strong – and strong means healthy.

Weighing in on the other side of the debate are those who work with unwell babies. In paediatric hospitals there is a common saying: 'A baby who is not growing is dying.' Growth occurs when a baby is able to take in more energy than they consume. If a baby is not getting enough milk, they may stay the same size or start to lose weight. It is important to remember that some babies are not taking in enough energy to grow. These babies need to be closely monitored to ensure that they have the energy and nutrients they require not only to grow, but to thrive.

There is a difference between a baby who is growing slowly along their own curve and a baby who has hit a plateau and stopped growing. Babies who are not growing at all, or who are losing weight, need to be closely monitored. If you look at the last measurements taken of your baby, it can be difficult to tell whether your baby is in a period of stasis (which could last anywhere from 2 to 28 days) or whether they have stopped growing. That is why your baby's growth trend is more important than any single measurement taken at a particular time. If you can feel that your baby has some fat underneath the skin of their upper arms, thighs and tummy, you can rest assured that they have fat stores available to fuel growth.

So, here is the takeaway message about growth: Feed your baby if they are hungry. Do not worry if they suddenly start feeding more than usual. When you go for your baby's scheduled vaccinations, get your baby weighed by the clinic sister. Use the growth charts as a general guide, but do not fret if your baby gains 100 g one week and 320 g the next. Short periods of no growth will happen. Periods of sudden growth will happen too.

Development

Development follows a similar pattern to growth: there are short periods of no apparent learning or skill acquisition followed by sudden periods of immense learning and change. Yesterday, your baby could not say 'mama', and suddenly today they can't stop saying it.

Development is also universal – all babies around the world follow a fairly consistent pace of skill acquisition over time. As discussed in the introduction, development is influenced by many factors, such as genetics, gestational age and environment, but despite these differences babies land up on a similar journey – after which we see them walking and talking as if they have always been doing so.

To study development, we have divided it into categories: gross motor, fine motor, communication and self-care skills. Gross motor covers movements of the large muscle groups (think rolling, crawling, standing and walking). Fine motor looks at the movements of small muscle groups (like those of the eyes and hand). Communication covers both what a baby hears and understands, as well as what a baby says (verbally and non-verbally). Self-care skill covers age-appropriate tasks (such as holding a cup, eating with a spoon, showing that your nappy is dirty).

These divisions help us with research as well as planning interventions. However, they are less useful for parents. When parents see developmental checklists, they generally focus on one or two items – usually the items their baby has not yet achieved. They may then try and practise that one skill so they can tick it off the list and move onto the next skill – the one just further up the ladder.

Viewing development as a ladder where one skill is gained before moving on to gain another can actually be a barrier to normal development. In reality, development is more like a bowl of spaghetti. Each skill is intricately wrapped up into another, and it is hard to see where one spaghetti strand starts and where another ends. In other words, every area of development affects every other area of development.

Here is an example. You may notice that your five-month-old baby cannot sit, so you decide to start practising sitting. Funnily enough, your baby was actually busy practising learning to sit while perfecting many things horizontally on the floor. If you don't see the point of all this rolling and pushing on the floor, then you will probably decide to pop your baby into a bouncy chair. You may feel better – your baby is sitting up and is entertained! But in reality, you have prevented your baby from learning how to sit, how to get into sitting and how to get out of sitting.

Sitting happens when there is balance and control between the tummy and back muscles. This balance is governed by the visual system, the balance system and the musculoskeletal system. So, a baby who is rolling and creeping and pushing up into sitting is actually working on sitting skills.

There are many other skills that rely on these systems too. You first need to use your hands and eyes together in midline horizontally before you can use your hands in upright sitting. The same can be said about speech. Many babies babble far more when moving around horizontally than when placed upright. So, when looking at your baby, try to identify what they are doing rather than focusing only on what they need to do next.

Each milestone is wonderful and does bring its own developmental benefits, but making it the most important thing in your baby's life will become a barrier to development rather than the stepping stone it was meant to be.

Remember, as neuroscientist Mijna Hadders-Algra has shown, 'Slow development of a single function usually has no clinical significance, but the finding of a general delay is clinically relevant.' This means that if your baby is doing really well in all areas but is just not doing one thing in one area (such as sitting), it is not going to hold your baby back. However, if you notice that your baby is struggling in more than one area (gross motor, fine motor, communication and self-care), it would be wise to consult a health professional who understands the importance of early intervention.

Babies whom I have seen benefit from early intervention include:

1. Babies who struggled to latch and breastfeed
2. Babies who have not been making communication attempts, such as smiling or babbling
3. Babies who have asymmetries, such as keeping their head turned to one side or using one hand or leg more than the other

4. Babies who have felt weak or floppy since birth and are now not showing a variety of movement patterns during floor time
5. Babies who have had a hard time tolerating different textures such as the carpet, grass, sand or body lotion
6. Babies who have pain during or after feeding
7. Babies who follow instructions beautifully but do not say any words
8. Babies who struggle to use their hands to grasp tools such as a spoon or small objects such as a piece of rope
9. Babies who struggle to take weight through their feet and legs
10. Babies who struggle to manage a variety of solid foods. There may be lots of gagging or vomiting.

What is early intervention?

Early intervention describes any intervention that occurs in the first 1 000 days of your baby's life with the intention of helping your baby grow and develop optimally. Early intervention includes any intervention that may bolster a child's development and can include nutrition, bonding, healthcare, therapies and/or assistive devices.

Nutritional interventions are provided by dietitians and speech language therapists. Dietitians decide what the best food would be for your baby and what quantity is needed – for example, how much milk as well as which milk or formula will suit your baby best. Speech language therapists, on the other hand, decide how your baby can eat each food safely. For example, some babies will be able to have solids orally but need to be fed milk via a nasogastric tube (a tube that goes from their nose down to their tummy to avoid swallowing).

Bonding interventions are provided by social workers and family psychologists. Social workers are experts in child rights and are able to support families by doing regular home visits and check-ins. They specialise in facilitating foster care and adoptions. Family psychologists usually focus more on helping parents adjust to their new roles, especially if there has been difficulty in bonding due to postnatal depression or any other mental health issue.

Healthcare interventions are provided by nurses and doctors. Nurses have regular contact with babies, checking their weight, growth and development. Doctors are called upon if medical or surgical intervention is needed for either the parent or the baby.

Therapies are provided by a multidisciplinary team. Physiotherapists can offer laser treatments for sore nipples and help with women's health issues post-delivery, such as incontinence and weak pelvic floor muscles. They also help when it comes to a baby's physical development. Occupational therapists use everyday activities to help babies who may be struggling with a developmental delay or with sleep or behavioural difficulties. Audiologists provide early screening for hearing impairments and fit hearing aids when required. Speech therapists help babies learn communication skills when needed.

Therapists issue assistive devices to babies when needed. These include things like orthotic footwear, hearing aids, specialised positioning equipment, splints, and adapted bottles and cups. These devices make it easier for babies to perform specific age-appropriate tasks like sit, stand, hear, drink and eat.

We know that a baby's brain is growing rapidly and making connections at an astonishing rate. Even a little change can have a big effect on the young brain, which is why early intervention is celebrated around the world.

If you are aware that your baby is struggling, you may want to seek support from one of these health professionals.

Kyle and Kelly's story

Early identification of a delay often means that the intervention needed is less intense and can happen over a shorter period. This is because the behaviour is less entrenched; it is often easier to show a younger child a new or different way of doing something than an older child.

Kyle and Kelly were non-identical twins born at 34 weeks. As is common with twins, one twin was developing more quickly than the other, and this concerned their parents. They were considered 'high-risk infants'. These are babies who require more than the standard monitoring and care offered to a healthy-full term newborn infant. They usually spend time in the NICU as they may have:

- Respiratory distress syndrome (they were born with immature lungs and require assistance to breathe)
- Apnoea (they forget to breathe, and therefore stop breathing for more than 20 seconds at a time)
- Hyperglycaemia (their sugar levels are too high)
- Congenital abnormalities (they may have heart, intestinal and brain conditions).

Babies are usually discharged from the NICU when they weigh 2 000 g and are able to breathe and feed independently.

At-risk or high-risk babies include:

- Babies born prematurely (before 37 weeks)
- Babies with a low birth weight (below 2 000 g)
- Multiples (twins, triplets etc.).

Kelly and Kyle were at risk as they were born six weeks prematurely and were twins. They also weighed less than 2 000 g. It was wise for their parents to bring them for a full developmental assessment when they were eight months old.

Their parents were correct. Kyle was developing within his corrected age band (remember, he was born six weeks early), but Kelly, who had had a rougher start, was behind in her gross motor, fine motor and language skills. Kyle was energetic and seemed to get to toys more quickly than Kelly did. Kelly appeared to be gaining less weight and was watching more than doing.

Kelly attended a few one-on-one therapy sessions and her parents were given a home programme to meet her specific needs. The home programme adapted the way in which her parents were doing everyday tasks (such as feeding, playing, bathing, dressing and nappy changes) to develop her gross motor, fine motor and language skills. They were asked to return after three months.

When the twins were 11 months old, they both returned. Another developmental assessment was completed within their new age band. I was overjoyed to see that both twins came out with scores around the 50th percentile in all skill areas.

I explained to their parents that the percentiles were how we as therapists knew which kids needed help and which were developing well on their own. Scoring on the 50th percentile would mean that Kelly and Kyle were doing better than 49 out of 100 babies their age. When using percentiles, any score between the 37th and 75th percentile is seen as 'average' and means the baby is developing age-appropriately.

What I found more shocking was their father's response. 'Average scores?' he said, as if it were a question. I could see he was not pleased. He asked for another home programme. I couldn't understand what for. When he said, 'I do not want my kids to be average. I want you to help them become above average. Could we get them to the 99th percentile?', I heard what so often goes unsaid.

Parents may try to create a 'superbaby' by pushing their baby to achieve skills earlier than appropriate. This goal-driven approach often results in rushing through 'less' important things – like taking time for free play or to develop emotional well-being.

Giving your baby extra healthy food and extra good sleep and extra stimulation may not make your baby extra special. Think of it like taking vitamins. Yes, there is a minimum amount that is required, otherwise ill health is likely. However, overdo it and you will create toxicity.

'Above average' should not be your goal in the first year.

Euan's story

The thing about being a parent is that there is always something to worry about. I got a call from my best friend, Kath. She had been googling. Her eight-week-old baby boy, who was exclusively breastfeeding, had gained an admirable 420 g since his last weight check . . . one week ago. He had gained nearly half a kilogram in one week!

Her greatest concern was, 'Is this normal?' Her Google journey had led her to a wide range of articles, some suggesting it was normal, some suggesting constipation and others suggesting gigantism.

There was nothing wrong with Euan. He had simply had an incredible growth spurt and was likely not to grow as much at the next few weigh-ins. What should have been a chance to celebrate (*yeah 420 g!*) became something worrying because it did not fit in with the average weight gain expected per week (usually about 140–200 g).

Being aware that leaps and spurts can happen should help you anticipate periods of rapid growth and periods of less growth. Remember that data is only useful when interpreted in context.

When you put data together, you start to notice trends. Trends are probably more useful than single data points; keep track of your baby's weight, but try to bring some perspective to each weigh-in.

REALITY 7: Your baby will grow and develop in spurts

- Growth charts are useful for spotting trends, especially to pick up whether a baby is not growing. A single measurement is less useful and shouldn't be used to draw any conclusions.
- Babies do not grow the same amount every day or every week. It is to be expected that your baby's needs are going to fluctuate from day to day and week to week.
- The most rapid growth happens in the first year of life – both physically and developmentally. This

means the first year is likely to be the most challenging for you and your baby. Cut yourself some slack!

- The first eight weeks of your baby's life is the time in which they will change most rapidly. This is why it can be hard to find a rhythm in those first two months. Don't worry if today is different from yesterday.

Don't worry if today is different from yesterday

Signs that you are busting Myth 7

✔ You no longer need to weigh your baby after every feed. You trust them to tell you when they are hungry and when they are full.

✔ Because growth and development happen in spurts, you expect their behaviour to change from time to time. You know there will be easier days and trickier days.

✔ You are taking your baby for the required health checks but are more interested in their weight trend than what their weight was on the day.

✔ You are proud of what your baby can do and are enjoying each stage of the first year, rather than rushing towards one milestone. You have embraced the fact that development is more like a bowl of spaghetti than like a ladder that needs to be climbed as quickly as possible.

✔ You have accepted that, as the Proud Owner of a Non-Unicorn Baby, your baby does not have to be a baby prodigy. Because 'superbaby' does not necessarily mean 'superperson'.

Myth 8
Your baby needs specialised stimulation classes and educational toys to thrive

The Unicorn Baby has a full and well-rounded extra-curricular programme. The Unicorn Baby attends swimming lessons on a Monday from 14:00–14:15 and can float happily on their back when submerged in the pool. The Unicorn Baby has always really enjoyed baby massage classes on a Tuesday from 09:00–09:30, falling asleep at the end and allowing their mother to enjoy a cup of coffee undisturbed with her new mom-friends. The Unicorn Baby shows up and coos cutely at the baby yoga class on a Wednesday from 12.00–12.45 and kicks their legs rhythmically during music ring on Thursdays from 16:00–16:30. The Unicorn Baby is interested in the educational toys they are given to play with, and would never grab hold of their mother's lipstick or smartphone. They know that baby toys are for them and everything else in the house is not. The Unicorn Baby is exceptionally well-educated and therefore developing just ahead of the curve. In every developmental area, of course.

Tackling Myth 8 is tricky, as many modern parents seem to have more faith in others than in themselves. Parents are outsourcing to 'experts' what used to be left to Mom and Dad. Their intentions are good: they want to bring out the best in their babies and are willing to sacrifice time, money and energy to do it. It makes sense, as many parents have chosen to have babies slightly later than their parents did in favour of excelling in their careers. The logic seems to be to find someone who is experienced to guide them through this unfamiliar terrain. Surely it can only be beneficial for a baby to attend regular training with an expert?

The answer to this, of course, is yes – as well as 'Hell, no!'

Yes, information is power. But no, you need to be careful what you choose to outsource and who you choose to outsource to when it comes to parenting.

Baby stimulation classes have really grown in popularity over the past decade. These classes can be hugely beneficial to new moms and dads who, in Western society, may find themselves caring for a new baby in isolation. Baby classes can be a place to gain emotional support from other parents who are in the same boat. Attending classes can also help a new parent feel more productive and successful when asked, 'So, what do you do all day?'

It can be the thing that gets you out the house, the thing you can plan your day around. It can also be a way to ensure that you know what your nanny is getting up to if you have returned to work.

However, I feel it is essential to warn parents who do not have a Unicorn Baby that your baby may not enjoy these outings – and, alas, neither may you. And that's okay.

Why? Because some babies hate swimming while you are watching them. They may feel happier being with you or not being in the water at all until they are much older. Many babies simply hate baby massage. The cues they give while their parent is massaging them show that they find it invasive. They don't want long strokes, or soft strokes, or any strokes at all.

Your baby may want to sleep during baby yoga, as this is when they feel tired. They may feel inspired to poo during music ring. Every. Single. Thursday. And while all these scenarios are highly annoying for parents and nannies everywhere who had got themselves and their baby dressed and out the house, you will have to accept that this is your baby's response to these activities.

Your response to these activities may also surprise you. You may not like the advice that gets thrust at you at these gatherings. You may also not like the constant barrage of personal questions that complete strangers could ask. You may hate handing your baby over to the yoga teacher or dislike being watched as you play and interact with your baby. That's okay too.

Give yourself permission to try new things and leave classes if they are not turning out to be very playful for you or your baby. In fact, give yourself permission to not leave the house at all if you can see it is going to be one of those days. An alternative could be to consider asking a family member to watch your baby while you attend a class. This way, you may be able to learn some new info and get to interact with the others without rubbing your baby up the wrong way. Although not bringing your baby along may rub some others up the wrong way – but hey, there's nothing you can or should do about that.

In reality, your baby may not always want to play when it is playtime. And that is normal.

Babies play when they are neither hungry, nor tired, nor annoyed. They play when their nappy is not soiled. They play when they are neither too hot nor too cold, when they are neither bored nor scared. They play when they are in their happy place, and this state sometimes lasts only a few minutes.

Signs that your baby does or does not want to play

Engagement cues are signals or body language your baby uses to show that they like what is going on around them. They are called approach or coping signals, and include the following:

- Eyes become wide open and bright as the baby focuses on you
- Turning eyes, head or body towards you or the person who is talking
- Alert face
- Healthy 'rosy' colour
- Steady breathing
- Hand-to-mouth activity, often accompanied by sucking movements

- Hands clasped together
- Grasping on to your finger or an object
- Smooth hand, arm and leg movement
- Softly flexed posture (looks relaxed).

Disengagement cues are signals or body language your baby uses to show that they do not like what is going on around them. These signals tell you when your baby is stressed and needs a break from what is happening. They are called defensive or avoidance signals, and include the following:

- Crying or fussing
- Gagging, spitting out
- Raised eyebrows
- Frowning, grimacing
- Hiccoughing, yawning, sneezing
- Becoming red, pale or mottled
- Irregular breathing
- Jittery or jerky movements
- Agitated or thrashing movements
- Falling asleep (this is the baby's way of shutting out the stimulus)
- Turning eyes, head or body away from you or the person who is talking
- Salute, finger splay
- Back arching.

In turn, how you respond is very important. Responding appropriately to your baby's disengagement cues helps your baby make sense of what they are feeling. It can also prevent your baby needing to communicate more forcefully – such as using back arching and screaming to say, 'I don't like this!'

If your baby shows disengagement cues, you may need to accept that today's class (or part of the class) is not for them. Trying to force a baby who is not up for it to participate clearly has no educational benefit, and will not do much for your mood either.

So, what should you do when you notice that your baby is in play mode?

Let's take a step back and redefine what you think play actually is.

Types of play

As with everything else, babies should be able to enjoy a variety of types of play, as well as a variety of types of toys. Let's look at the various types of play that your baby will enjoy, and what makes a great toy.

'Do babies really need all this stuff?' is probably the comment I enjoy hearing most at baby showers. In reality, babies do need many things, like blankets and clothes and nappies, but they don't need many toys, especially in the first year.

There are so many cool and cute products available that it makes it difficult for new parents to know what they really need and what could turn out to be clutter. Many families are trying to move away from plastics, where possible, and to live in a more energy-efficient way, downscaling their homes and vehicles. Cities are booming, house prices are up and so many young families are living in smaller spaces – out of choice for some, and out of necessity for others.

If you grew up in a large family home but are planning to raise your baby in a smaller space, you may be feeling a little more anxious than others about where all this baby stuff is going to go. To reassure you, it is becoming increasingly rare for families to have a dedicated playroom. Your baby will be just fine without one, but you may find it difficult to start sharing your space with your baby's stuff.

The good news is that you may need less of this stuff than you thought you would. Let's look at what babies actually *need*.

Babies need nutrition, love, security and stimulation. They do not *need* toys, although there are many toys that can help you provide stimulation.

So, what do you need to do to stimulate your baby? The good news is that it is not all up to you. Your healthy baby is going to seek out stimulation. They are going to want to check out all kinds of things. As developmental expert Mary Sheridan says, 'It is in the nature of the developing body to be continuously active, the developing mind to be intensely curious and of the developing personality to seek good relationships with others.'

Your baby is going to be on a mission to discover. Some of this will involve toys, but mostly they will be discovering people, everyday objects, and experiences.

People

Babies love people. They love being picked up and looking at faces. Babies think faces are the best – especially the faces of those they love and trust. People can count as toys. The people who are a part of your daily life will provide opportunities for your baby to play and learn.

This could be great news if you have a large tribe. However, it may put more pressure on you if you spend most of your time with just your baby. It can feel overwhelming being so popular and in demand, but it is a very healthy sign if your baby is seeking you out. Remember, your baby wants to develop a relationship with you. The way babies do this is by playing with you.

Everyday objects

Babies love everything they see you touch. Your stuff is cool. Shoes, handbag, keys, gate remote, phone . . . this is all the good stuff, the contraband that they are told *not to touch*. Allowing your baby to fiddle with everyday objects that you deem safe is a great way to provide stimulation without needing to buy more stuff. The kitchen is full of toys – wooden spoons for banging, Tupperware for stacking, metal spoons for clanking, cups and jugs for pouring . . . you get the idea.

You may want to go through your home and put together a basket or drawer of everyday stuff in each room that is 'baby approved'. This way, your baby may play with silky scarfs, wooden-bead necklaces and fuzzy slippers while you are getting dressed. If there is nothing to explore, or what you have provided is no longer that enthralling, your baby may become more interested in getting to the plug points and water taps. Don't worry – this, too, shall pass.

Experiences

Babies love learning through experiences. When we hear 'experiences', we think seven-night-stay-on-an-exotic-island. Babies are slightly easier to please. A new experience for a baby could be sitting in the wheelbarrow while you rake leaves. It could be going to the shop to buy milk. Providing experiences for your baby does not need to follow a well-thought-out plan. Babies learn through doing life with you. They see chores as play. They see visiting a grandparent's home like you view taking a space shuttle.

You can use the ordinary things to teach your baby lots of extraordinary lessons. Babies love sensorimotor experiences, and fortunately these happen all the time.

Much-loved baby adventures include:

- Taking a walk or run in the pram
- Visiting a pretty garden, river, pond or beach
- Taking a trip to a petting zoo or animal farm
- Watching the sun come up
- Looking at the moon and stars
- Putting bird food in the garden and watching the birds come to eat
- Seeing the rubbish truck come and collect the bins
- Washing the car with soapy bubbles
- Spotting an aeroplane or helicopter in the sky
- Throwing a ball for a dog
- Swinging at the park.

How to spot a great toy

Cas Holman is a toy designer. She spent much of her career designing toys only to realise that her product was really play. She has witnessed how children enjoy complexity and creativity. Her goal has been to create play experiences, rather than playthings. I love how she says, 'Kids are pretty sophisticated . . . when you're a kid easy is boring.' I would say babies are pretty sophisticated too.

Cas has discovered something that many parents have discovered about their babies: babies are more interested in people and everyday objects than they are in their expensive toys. As we all observe at Christmas, babies are often more entranced by the box that the toy came in than by the toy itself.

Why is this? What needs to be present for play to happen? What makes a great toy great? Spoiler alert: it's often not the toys you bought, sterilised and put on your baby's play mat.

A great toy is fun

No one likes doing boring things. Play needs to be fun. The things your baby is playing with should make them smile and giggle. For example, putting on a hat and covering up your eyes can become a hilarious game of peek-a-boo. Putting on lipstick and kissing a mirror or each other can result in fits of laughter. When your baby sees a toy, they should be excited to play with it. If they are completely disinterested, you may have got a dud.

Remember, your baby should be driven to play and interact more with you than with toys. Take wooden ABC blocks, for example. If you place your baby on the floor surrounded by a pile of blocks and walk off, there will be some exploratory play – perhaps some mouthing and some grasping of the blocks – but your baby may get tired of that.

However, if you were to join in the play, get onto the ground and show your little one how, when you put a block into a tin, it makes a lovely bang, they may love doing this over and over again with you. You could also show them how to build a tower or a train or sing a song while banging the blocks together in a rhythmical pattern. Play is going to last longer and be far more fun for your baby when it is more complex, more surprising, more exciting.

Try placing one, two, three blocks on top of one another in front of your baby and then saying, 'Ready, steady, boom!' to show them how the blocks fall down. Some babies end up in fits of giggles as they anticipate knocking the tower over and seeing your face, aghast with surprise, afterwards.

A great toy is motivating

Play is driven by your baby's curiosity or desire to know more and do more. Play is sustained when your baby sees that there is more to discover than they initially imagined.

Toys that are highly motivating for babies usually involve movement. Babies love moving and are trying to conquer gravity themselves. Any toy that moves when they move is always a hit. Think about mobiles that swing and shake when babies swipe at them; small and large balls that roll and bounce, windmills or fans that move in the air, and bubbles that are there one moment and the next – poof! – they just disappear. These items will make your baby feel more motivated to swipe, reach, throw, fetch, blow and pop, over and over again.

A great toy is activating

Playing with a toy should activate or 'paint' your baby's sensorimotor cortex. The more a toy helps to light up the cortex, the more engaging it is. What lights up the sensorimotor cortex? Anything that your baby touches, smells, tastes, hears, or sees. In addition, anything that entices your baby to move, or that moves your baby, is going to activate the motor cortex.

Your baby will love playing with coloured macaroni in a plastic bottle, especially if the lid goes on and off; they will love pushing and pulling a little boat along the surface of the water in the bath; they will take great pleasure in picking apart flowers from your garden, and in squishing through jelly to find wooden animals. If play engages your baby's senses, what they are playing with will be a great toy.

A great toy allows exploration

Babies love exploring. At first, their world is limited to their own body and their parents, but soon enough they start to want to explore the world beyond this. From birth to six months, babies love exploring their own little bodies. A toy that allows them to learn more about their body parts is always a winner. Babies love having interesting socks on their feet. Sew a small bell on to the sock to make it even more enticing. Babies love dipping their hands into body cream and lathering themselves from head to toe. They will happily roll on grass, and enjoy it when you blow raspberries on their tummies. A toy that does not allow a baby to learn more about themselves may not be played with as much.

From seven to twelve months, a baby will start moving about to try to discover what is out there. They become mobile and enjoy climbing on and off, up and down, and in and out of everything. Your baby may love going for walks, want to touch and mouth everything they see, and want to try out all the apparatus at the park. They may be fascinated by rain and rustling leaves and cats that dash out of reach. A toy that promotes exploration of the outside world, such as gumboots, a wagon, spade and bucket set, or a book about a great adventure, are sure to become favourites.

A great toy extends play, rather than defining it

Play morphs. What I mean by this is that play may start at one point and then move through a series of transitions. Toys that extend play will be played with and learnt from far more than toys that dictate that there is only one way to play.

Let's take a wagon, for example. Play could start with you putting your baby into a low wooden wagon and pushing them up and down the passage. This game could go on for a few minutes until your baby decides they want to try to push. They climb out; you help them hold the wagon, and step slowly down the passage. Perhaps they are too wobbly and this is less fun then they thought it would be, so they plonk down onto their bottom and remove their shoes. They place them inside the wagon and start looking for other things they can put in. Suddenly, the wagon is a basket. After filling the wagon, they start handing items out. After each item is handed to you, you give them a kiss to say thank you for that awesome shoe or cuddly bear. When the wagon is empty they turn it upside down and start banging on the wooden base and on the wheels. They like to see how the base stays still but the wheels turn when you touch them.

The wagon supported and promoted many types of play, instead of having only one directive. A toy that extends play is always going to be played with far more than a toy that does not. It is often electronic toys that define and limit play. Toys such as a robotic dog that takes some steps and barks when switched on are fascinating the first few times you see it come alive, but they quickly lose their appeal when you learn you can't cuddle it or plop it into the bath.

A great toy allows a baby to fail, fail and fail again

Some toys intrinsically call for failure. They are not designed for success at the first attempt. This is important because babies need to learn which strategies work well and which do not. They need to refine their movement patterns and get rid of the patterns that are less useful as they grow.

A simple shape-sorter ball requires your baby to pick up a shape and try to match it to the corresponding hole. Your baby will need to try over and over again, using various grasps and various planes of movement, to push the shape through successfully. Your baby will definitely fail the first few attempts. That's more than okay – that's learning.

On the other hand, a walking ring offers babies immediate success. Once inside, any movement will propel them forward. It is unlikely that your baby would ever be unsuccessful in using this toy. This means that your baby will have fewer learning opportunities when in the walking ring then they would have when out of the walking ring.

Each time you are ready to buy your baby some new toys, ask yourself these five questions:

1. Is it motivating and fun?
2. Is it activating?
3. Does it promote exploration?
4. Does it extend play?
5. Does it allow for failure?

If you can say yes to most of these questions, you are guaranteed to have found a great toy that will help you and your baby play and learn.

How to play in the first year

So, now you know how to pick the toys – but how do you use them? Are you a mom who feels you just don't know how to play while your baby is not saying or doing much? Or are you one of the many dads whose concern is that the games that come naturally, like roughhousing, are too rough and will hurt your small baby?

Much has been written about what *not* to do in the first year of your baby's life, most of it geared to accomplish a noble outcome – survival. But very little has been said about how to play with a baby. Parents are uncertain whether they should be exposing their baby to stimulation programmes or keeping them at home to protect their delicate, immature, neurological system from over-stimulation.

The good news is that it's not as complicated as you may have been led to believe – and that, fortunately, it takes very little to make a big impact. Here's how to play with your baby during the first year. For the days shall be long, but the years shall be short!

1. **Look out for times when your baby wants to play, rather than trying to enforce a fixed playtime.** Your baby may draw you in with their eyes, or smile, or coo, or babble when they see you. They are really saying, 'Hey, come and play.' As you respond to their cues, they learn that, when they give these signals, you respond in a certain way. This interaction helps your baby gain self-esteem, trust and communication skills.

2. **Redefine what you call 'play'.** Play may last five seconds or five minutes, depending on your baby's age and level of interest. Often, as parents we want an end product (or at least a really cute video to upload), but for babies the experience is what really matters. Blowing raspberries, ripping up a newspaper, discovering their toes . . . the first year is a series of experiments. Your baby is discovering new sensations and movements, and often all they want is for you to be near them as they make these discoveries. Looking together is called 'joint attention'. It is the beginning of developing concentration skills. Playing with your baby is really just introducing them to the big, wide world.

3. **You are the best toy you could ever buy your baby.** It turns out that if you want to give your baby the best chance at developing *any* skill, playing with you is the best chance they have. Motor skills? You. Emotional skills? You. Social skills? You! Many parents think it is exposure to a variety of toys that helps their baby learn, when in fact it is exposure to their parents in a variety of situations that makes their neurons fire. Your baby needs you to roll, munch, crawl, laugh, sing, rock, touch, talk, move, laugh, make funny faces, play peek-a-boo and clean up alongside them. And no, this does not require you to be playful all day long, but rather to be ready for play if the fun should find you.

4. **Playing should be fun for you too.** There is a Finnish proverb which, roughly translated, says: 'Those things you learn without joy you will forget easily.' Every parent wants

their baby to develop rock-solid emotional and social skills. Playing together and really enjoying each other is the beginning of this journey. So, if you find yourself feeling lost at home, with little inspiration for play, take your baby's lead and see whether you both enjoy any of the following sensorimotor games that happen to be activities that you do every day anyway:

- Jump in the bath together and see what happens when you add bubble bath, crunchy Epsom salts, sponges and slimy baby soap.
- Put on a silly hat or mask the next time you are dressing your baby. Give them a turn to make funny faces and hide.
- Lie down on your tummies facing each other and enjoy making a yummy mess of picnicking.
- Prefer sitting or standing to eat? Go for it! Have a selection of smooth- and rough-textured favourites (apple sauce, banana slices, yoghurt, chocolate pudding, teething biscuits, etc.) and see what happens when you eat them, smear them, lick them. You get the picture.

When play is joyful, magical things happen for both a baby's development and the parent-child bond. So, don't aim to get in 60 minutes of play each day. Take each day as it comes and see how you can steal these moments of joy from the ordinary. It is amazing how much your baby will learn about following instructions, packing away, counting numbers, greeting strangers, dealing with upsets and taking turns through these simple interactions.

When will my baby start playing on their own?

Many parents ask me, 'How long should I aim to play with my baby for each day?' Often, the other side of this question is this: 'When is it okay for me to leave my baby to play on their own? And for how long?'

The answer to all of these questions is a delicate matter, as each family is made up of distinctly different characters who all have their own way of playing. Some are introverts and some extroverts. Some will enjoy physical activities (like wrestling) and others will enjoy more sedentary activities (like reading). As I mentioned before, for play to be fun it needs to be fun for all who are playing. Faking enjoyment won't suffice.

On the other hand, all parents find themselves in this predicament: they need to get some stuff done and they can't be playing with their baby all day. To this, I say – of course! But while a baby who can play independently is a wonderful thing, there is also a need to help your baby play alongside and with other people. While we are focused on cultivating independence, we can sometimes forget about how interdependent we all really are.

Babies will play alone as well as with others in a variety of ways as they move through the stages of play. Each stage of a baby's development will offer different challenges when it comes to your getting stuff done.

Let's look at the various types of play that a baby will enjoy in their first year. You'll find some ideas that show play can be very simple indeed.

1. **Social play.** This is the earliest form of play and can even be seen in newborns. It is how babies practise communication and social interaction. Between birth and three months, babies will smile during face-to-face interactions, coo in

response to playful interactions, and notice and respond to different tones in your voice. Between four and six months, babies will play peek-a-boo, and laugh and smile at themselves in a mirror.

At about nine months, you may notice a big change. Your baby will stop wanting to interact with everybody and seem to have a favourite person – the only person they want to be held by or played with. This is normal, and a great sign of secure attachment. Your baby will slowly widen their social circle again – just give them some time. It is cute that it is around the same time that your baby will start to shake their head for 'no' – telling strangers very clearly to back off.

Social play is responsible for attunement. Attunement is when a parent and a baby synchronise and seem to interact in a sort of harmony. They get each other, and it just seems easy. A baby who can fit into a family and participate in social games will find it easier to take on all the conscious and subconscious social rules that govern a family. Social play helps babies understand that what they do and how they feel has an effect on those around them.

2. **Sensorimotor play.** This is probably the easiest type of play to recognise as a parent. It involves the senses (sight, smell, taste, touch and hearing), as well as movement. Some parents will absolutely love sensorimotor play, and others won't. And that's okay.

Sensorimotor play is a great way to tap into both the sensory homunculus and the motor homunculus (see mouthing for more information).

Popular sensorimotor games include:

- Watching and popping bubbles
- Kicking your legs to move a balloon
- Smearing paint on a table
- Swinging back and forth
- Digging in sand
- Playing with musical toys
- Having a bubble bath.

Sensorimotor play will hold a baby's attention, but it requires supervision as babies often get in over their heads when it comes to messy play.

3. **Parallel play.** This is one of the sweetest types of play. Those playing are next to each other but not interacting with one another. For example, you are in the kitchen cooking supper and your baby is sitting on the floor playing with a pot and a spoon, pretending to cook alongside you. Or you are texting on your phone and your baby grabs the TV remote, sits next to you and pretends to text too. Parallel play allows a baby to learn from others without having to deal with them interfering in their game.

4. **Solitary play.** Oh, to have a baby who is happy to play on their own! Now *that* should be a developmental milestone. Yes, playing alone is an important skill – but many babies seem to need their mom or dad all the time. This is quite normal. Babies need your attention to learn and grow. You are their first friend, their source of food and love, their security guard, their bus and tour guide on this grand adventure of life. Babies who are neither tired nor hungry nor wanting your attention will play happily on their own for a while.

But be warned: a baby who is playing quietly on their own is usually a baby who is involved in some seriously messy play. Some horror stories include finding your baby playing with their own vomit, smearing poop all over their cot, or pouring a full bottle of milk all over their head and clothes.

Don't worry – there are some happier solitary play scenarios:

- Baby lies on their back exploring their feet.
- Baby is placed on a play mat on their tummy and looks and squeals at various toys.
- Baby rests in a bouncy chair and kicks their legs to move back and forth.
- Baby rests on their back under a tree, watching the light move through the leaves.
- Baby enjoys listening to familiar nursery rhymes while rolling around in their cot.
- Baby sits in a box, fiddling with some ribbons.

You will be surprised at how quickly the time passes when caring for a young baby. On some days it will be easier to get through your list; on others it may be impossible, as your baby appears to just need you more. There is no such thing as 'spoiling' a baby. Giving your young baby lots of attention will not make them 'used to it' or 'need you more'.

The more people there are in a family, the more the workload can be divided up – at least prior to the nine-month mark, at which point your baby will have a clear preference for one person. Remember, this is just a season. The 'needy' stage does not last forever. Soon, your baby will be crawling, walking and eventually running away from you. The more you put in, the more both of you will get out.

How to get more stuff done with your baby

- Baby wearing (using a baby sling or a blanket to secure your baby to your body) is a great way to free your hands, at home and when out shopping. Find a sling or baby system that feels right to you.
- Try to avoid using devices to distract your baby. Rather set up baby-friendly boxes or baskets in each room. Guidelines require no screen time for babies before they are 24 months old. That's right – none! For more information about screen time, have a look at Myth 10.
- If your baby loves sitting in their pram, you should be able to run more errands.
- Alternatively, stay in and use online banking and online shopping to help you get your errands done without all the packing and unpacking.
- Ask for help. Find your tribe and don't be afraid to ask them for help if you have an urgent deadline.

- A friendly pet or child can make a great playmate for your baby.

The story of the Good Doctor

My work life provides many opportunities to work alongside other health professionals. For many years, I worked alongside a brilliant paediatrician. She was the person you wanted to have on speed dial if you had young children. She was the person on my speed dial, for goodness' sake – and I had a whole whack of doctors to choose from.

The Good Doctor asked me to do a house visit after her first child was born. She was a beautiful full-term baby, and her mom was well aware of how lucky she was to have had a healthy child. Most successful professionals put a lot of pressure on themselves to be successful parents – except they often do not know what that should look like.

It was at this house visit that the Good Doctor explained: 'I know exactly what to do if a child is sick, what steps to follow and what signs to look for. But a healthy baby . . . what do you do with them when they *aren't* sick?'

We discussed a series of health-promoting postures and helpful products that she could use with her new baby, and then we hit shaky ground. How was she going to actually play with her baby? She was a tall, elegant woman who wore long skirts and dangly earrings. She was not the type of mom you would expect to find up to her elbows in homemade finger paint. Should she push through and knuckle down and force herself to play each day? Down on the floor, the way that she had seen many paediatric therapists do at the hospital?

My answer to her was no. Faking it was not the way forward. I reminded her: 'You are learning about your baby as much as she is learning about you.'

The Good Doctor may not have been into rough-and-tumble or messy play, but she had a wicked sense of humour and was fantastically musical. I encouraged her to share these with her baby. She could use her many songs and find many ways to laugh – in doing so, she would, in fact, be playing with her baby. And it would be authentic, not forced.

Her daughter went on to love music and dance, and had a flair for the dramatic – just like her mother. Don't worry, she got enough rough and tumble from her dad and messy play from her nanny. The Good Doctor made sure of that.

REALITY 8: You and your baby are not always going to want to play when it is playtime, and that is normal – your baby will learn from you, from everyday objects and from experiences

- The Unicorn Baby loves every baby class out there, but your baby may not always want to play or enjoy the class when it is playtime. This is normal.
- Your baby will give you signals to show you whether they are enjoying or not enjoying certain activities. Listen to these.
- There are four important aspects of playing in the first year: look out for times when your baby wants to play, rather than trying to enforce a fixed playtime; redefine what you call 'play' – aim for five seconds of

shared joy per day; you are the best toy you could ever buy your baby, so give your baby time rather than stuff; playing should be fun for you too.

- If you want to buy a great toy, ask yourself these five questions: Is it motivating and fun? Is it activating? Does it promote exploration? Does it extend play? Does it allow for failure?

Listen to your baby's signals

Signs that you are busting Myth 8

✔ You know when your baby wants to play.

✔ You have mastered a few games that suit their developmental stage. Peek-a-boo, anyone?

✔ You can list three things that your baby likes to play – for example, putting a warm face cloth on their tummy in the bath and taking it off again, talking to their elephant soft toy, and having raspberries blown on their palm.

✔ You and your baby are getting one dose of shared joy each day.

Myth 9
Your baby must do tummy time for 20 minutes every day

The Unicorn Baby never misses tummy time. They just love lying on their tummy on the floor for 20 minutes every day from 08:00–08:20 while their mother does her make-up. They push up on their arms without much fuss and never bang their head on the floor. They can play with a bunch of toys without any encouragement. They will roll at four weeks, sit at six months and crawl at eight months. They are the Unicorn Baby, after all.

If you're a new parent, I'm pretty sure you have already come across the phrase 'tummy time'. This term was coined to encourage parents to put their babies onto their tummies for play. It's a great idea, but why did parents have to be told to do this?

Parents had stopped putting their babies to sleep on their tummies because of the Back to Sleep campaign that was launched in 1994 in the USA by the National Institute of Child Health and Human Development, and later relaunched in 2009 as the Safe to

Sleep campaign. The Safe to Sleep campaign was implemented in countries as far flung as the Netherlands and New Zealand. These campaigns aimed to help reduce the incidence of Sudden Infant Death Syndrome (SIDS), and they did just that.

SIDS is the sudden death of an infant that remains unexplained despite post-mortem studies and death scene investigation. It is probably the worst scenario many parents can imagine: putting your healthy newborn to sleep only to find they have died an hour later. While it is incredibly rare, it is also incredibly devastating for families.

As the field of sleep science has grown, it has been possible to find out more about why SIDS may occur and why a baby who is sleeping on their back is less likely to become a SIDS victim. In 2003, Kahn and others, recorded 20 000 infants during one night in a paediatric sleep laboratory. Among these infants, some eventually died of SIDS. Looking back at the recordings of healthy infant sleep compared to those who had died of SIDS, it becomes clear that SIDS is not a simple phenomenon and is caused by multiple factors.

These factors are:

1. **Maturational processes.** SIDS victims may have brain-stem or cortical differences, which impair their ability to regulate autonomic functions such as maintaining a healthy body temperature and regular breathing.
2. **Medical conditions.** SIDS victims often have a medical history of obstructive sleep apnoea or a prior life-threatening event before death occurs. SIDS victims appear to stop breathing or hold their breath during sleep more often than healthy infants do.

3. **Environmental factors.** Some environmental factors increase a baby's risk of SIDS, such as a cold room temperature, the presence of cigarette smoke and parental use of illegal drugs and alcohol. Other environmental factors that are known to be protective include rooming in, breast-feeding and dummy use.

All three of these factors could contribute to SIDS, either independently or in combination. They all lead to the same series of events that result in a baby being less likely to wake from sleep and less able to maintain a healthy heart rate.

It is suspected that when babies sleep on their backs they arouse more easily and so are less likely to stop breathing. It is also thought that this position prevents babies from overheating or suffocating on soft bedding. Hence, authorities have asked all parents to put their babies to sleep on their backs in a cot with no bedding preferably in the parents' room. Of course, many parents battle to follow this advice as culture has a great influence on sleep practices.

Prior to the Safe to Sleep campaign, many babies spent much time sleeping on their stomachs – on their parents' bodies and in their cots. When they woke up, they would be able to experience movement in a variety of ways. As a journal article by Majnemer and Barr shows, as more babies began sleeping on their backs and having inadequate opportunities to move on their stomachs, there was an increase in the occurrence of delayed gross motor skills by the age of six months.

As Feijen and others note in a journal article, there has also been an increase in the occurrence of positional skull deformities in healthy infants such as brachycephaly (a flat spot at the back of the head) and plagiocephaly (a flat spot on one side of the head).

The bones of a baby's skull are soft, and mould over time. A baby who is often on their back looking up will have a flat spot on the back of their head. A baby who lies with their head turned to one side will have a flat spot on that side of their head.

Due to these concerns, new recommendations were added to the Safe To Sleep campaign:

1. At night, ensure that you alternate the side to which your baby is facing when they are asleep on their back. Alternate as follows: night 1 – head at top of cot; night 2 – head at bottom of cot.
2. During the day, get your baby to do tummy time on the floor.

The amount of tummy time prescribed was 20 minutes. The problem is that many babies who are not used to being on their stomachs hate being put there, especially on the floor. And especially for 20 minutes. Unfortunately, so many parents believed so whole-heartedly that it was good for their babies that they were willing to leave them there to cry for 20 minutes every day. It's no surprise that these babies acquired a serious dislike for this position. The reality is that your baby needs more than just tummy time to develop good postural control.

Development of postural control

While many parents simplify gross motor development into a three-step process of sit–crawl–walk, it is really more elaborate than that; the important bits lie in the dashes rather than in the sitting, crawling, or walking. The main goal of the first year is to gain postural control to conquer gravity.

Conquering gravity begins at birth and continues into our adult years. *In utero*, by 24–26 weeks of age babies have a fully developed brain that allows them to interpret sensory information from their environment (touch, taste, smell, hearing and vision) and produce all the movement patterns that they need to survive outside of the womb (including sucking, breathing, crawling and walking). These movements are extraordinarily vivid on an ultra-sound and well described by uncomfortable expectant moms. Those on the 'outside' love nothing more than to feel one of these jolts that confirm that a real-life baby is growing on the inside.

However, in the last trimester your baby grows so quickly that while all these movements are still possible from a neurological perspective, some become impossible thanks to the baby's cramped quarters. Your baby's joints stiffen in this 'fetal position', giving pressure into their joints that helps them to interpret where they are in space. It also gives them a mechanical advantage at birth when they first meet the paralysing force of gravity.

Once born, they do not need to learn to move, but rather how to move in the presence of gravity.

These large, crumpled-up babies are born with their heads, hands and feet close to their centre and can remain in this position whether placed on their backs or tummies. In the first three months after birth, they show off an ever-expanding repertoire of movement. To name just a few, babies can place their hands in their mouths, their arms under their chests, lift their heads off a surface, place their toes in their hands, and kick their legs and throw their arms around fanatically in all sorts of ways.

It's cute to watch, but what we often miss is that, during this time – while playing horizontally and supposedly doing little more than eating and sleeping – babies are preparing to succeed against gravity and go vertical. Rather than focusing on helping their babies to sit up or crawl or walk, parents could give their babies time to play in a variety of positions on the floor or on their parents' bodies where the emphasis is on free movement, sensorimotor play and self-discovery.

Thinking in 3D rather than 2D

A baby has trunk muscles that wrap around their body (as do you). The trunk muscles are found on their front, back and sides. Babies need to build all their trunk muscles to conquer gravity. Tummy time helps to build the muscles at the back of the trunk. There are other static positions, such as side lying and back lying, that are important too. Lying on their back, a baby strengthens the muscles on the front of their trunk. Lying on their side, a baby learns to switch on the side trunk muscles.

After conquering these three static positions, your baby learns to do something even more useful: they learn to move between them. Rolling is the first transitional movement, helping a baby move from back to front and front to back. And where do these transitional movements happen? The only place a baby can perform varied movements and continue to develop postural control is on the floor. That is why floor time, rather than just tummy time, is so important.

Development of sensory processing skills

The time on the floor (or lying on any firm surface, such as a parent's chest, the grass or a mat) promotes movement and weight-bearing, which gives your baby a variety of sensory experiences. This helps them to develop sensory processing skills such as:

- **Proprioception.** This develops through pressure on and in the baby's joints and muscles, and helps them know where they are in space.

- **Vestibular processing.** This develops through the movement of the fluid in the inner ear, and helps them gain balance and agility.
- **Tactile processing.** This develops through touching and mouthing different surfaces, and helps them to know if something is pleasant and useful or dangerous and better avoided. It also gives them a sense of where their body starts and ends.
- **Visual processing.** This develops through seeing objects near and far, as well as while lying and moving in different positions.

Each posture and movement will give your baby a different sensory experience. A variety of sensory experiences will give your baby the opportunity to learn sensory processing skills.

Development of perceptual skills

Being able to lie and roll, and push up in different postures, gives the brain a chance to develop many perceptual skills such as:

- **Body awareness** as your baby learns how big, high, long and wide they are
- **Left–right discrimination** as your baby learns that they have a left and a right side and goes on to establish a dominant side
- **Depth perception** as your baby learns how far away the floor and toys are from them by reaching towards these items, and also by bumping their head on the floor.

Again, the greater the variety of positions and sensory experiences, the easier it will be for your baby to learn perceptual skills. So yes, tummy time is super-duper beneficial but so are other positions and experiences. What your baby needs is to explore a variety of positions and attempt active movements on the floor.

But what happens if your baby hates it?

So, you've read all about how wonderful floor time is for your baby, got your camera ready and placed your little one on their side on the floor, and all you get is wailing? And now you're panicking that your baby is never going to make the goal of 20 minutes per day, which is sure to mean no crawling – and a life doomed to scholastic failure?

Relax. Despite floor time being so darn good for your baby, you may find that they do not like it at all. Medical conditions aside, most babies hate floor time as they hate being away from their parents' bodies, especially in the first three months.

To learn, babies need to feel safe as much as they need to play in a variety of positions to develop a variety of movement patterns. Don't ignore your baby's protests; instead, try some of the useful exercises that support their postural control.

The solution is that floor time does not have to start on the floor. Let's look at a no-cry approach to finding a variety of ways in which your baby can develop postural control.

Here are just a few no-floor positions that babies love at my occupational therapy practice. They all make use of your body. This is the best place to start to help your baby learn to conquer gravity:

Use your body, not the floor

1. **Seeing eye to eye**. There is no object more attractive to a baby than the human face. And there is nothing more comforting than a parent's face. This makes spending time looking at your face and hearing your voice highly moti-

vating and enjoyable for your baby. If your baby cannot tolerate much time in this first position (on their chest), offer them rest breaks by rolling them onto their back (lying on your lap).

Moving them gently from the one position to the other is a great way for them to experience face-to-face interaction in a variety of positions. The more upright you are, the easier it is for them. The more you lie down, the harder it will be for them.

2. **Sibling love.** As much as your baby will love you, they will also have a special love and interest in their siblings and pets. You can use this position to play a game of peek-a-boo,

stroke your dog or read a book to your older children. You can adjust the angle of your legs to make it more or less challenging for your baby. Some babies also love lying on their sibling's chest, which has the added benefit of sibling bonding. Obviously, lots of supervision will be needed!

3. **Monkeying around.** You can carry your baby around lying on your arm (in side lying or in tummy lying). They may even fall asleep like this. Monkeying around is a very comforting position for babies with abdominal cramps and reflux. This has the additional benefit of making your arms super strong too!

No-cry floor time

Once it is clear that your baby is showing interest not just in faces but in toys, you can start playing with them on the floor with these toys. A great way to do this is on a large, firm floor mat that is not slippery and does not 'gather' if your baby pulls at it. You may have a great heavy rug in your lounge or a suitable heavy picnic blanket that will work well.

1. **Back to basics.** Your baby needs time on the floor lying flat on their back too. Back lying is an important place to develop core muscle strength, as well as to continue

learning to roll. Many baby containers (such as car chairs, prams and bouncy chairs) can get in the way of your baby learning to conquer gravity from this position.

2. **Getting nosey.** Both of you lie on your tummies nose to nose, and either play with each other or interact with an inspiring toy or leaf or ball that sits between you. Reaching forward to grab your nose or a toy requires even more postural control, so you should encourage this. If your baby shows discomfort, be sure to show them how they can roll out of this position to spend some time on their back or side.

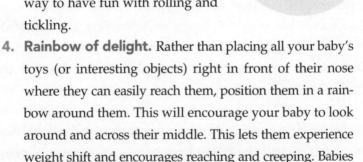

3. **Two sides to every story.** You and your baby have two sides – a right side and a left side. Side lying is a wonderful place to play and it's also a wonderful way to have fun with rolling and tickling.

4. **Rainbow of delight.** Rather than placing all your baby's toys (or interesting objects) right in front of their nose where they can easily reach them, position them in a rainbow around them. This will encourage your baby to look around and across their middle. This lets them experience weight shift and encourages reaching and creeping. Babies move because of what they see. Most babies start moving

because they want something that is out of reach.

We have examined the three major horizontal positions on the floor: tummy time, back lying and side lying. The floor has offered your baby stability, feedback and a chance to play with movement rather than learning how to play if placed in a particular position. Next, we look at the three major vertical positions. These happen to be the three most celebrated milestones in a baby's life – sitting, crawling and walking.

Sitting

Sitting up is the first 'big' gross motor milestone. It happens between six and ten months of age. To get into true, independent sitting, babies need to conquer gravity in smaller bits. They need to be able to:

- Push their chests off the ground (at about four months old)
- Roll from side to side (at about four and a half months old)
- Push themselves from side lying into sitting (at about six to nine months old).

Babies will sit up first in an assisted way – held up either by their parents hands, or by a device or by cleverly placed cushions. Giving a baby support can give them a taste of what it's like to be upright. There is nothing wrong with this; however, your baby will also need time learning to sit unassisted. Again, this will happen on the floor.

Your baby will start by prop sitting (here, their legs are straight and wide open, their arms out to prop them up like a tent) and then they tackle true sitting (here, they learn to hold themselves upright using their trunk muscles and rely less and less on their arms to prop themselves up).

The benefits of sitting

- **Vision.** A baby who can sit can see and make sense of the world in a different orientation.
- **Social interaction.** A baby can attract more attention and have more verbal interaction.
- **Digestion.** Both milk and solid foods are more likely to stay in their stomach, rather than coming back up.
- **Hand use.** A baby can use their hands to explore and mouth and clap rather than to hold their body up.

It is no coincidence that, at about the same time they are pushing up from their tummy to four-point kneeling. The same arm and trunk muscles they were using to hold themselves up against gravity in sitting have allowed them to learn how to hold the puppy position. Your baby is getting ready for the second 'big' gross motor milestone – crawling.

Crawling

Crawling is your baby's first taste of moving independently. It's like getting the keys to the car. You can go where you could never go before! This can be both exhilarating and terrifying for you and your baby.

Crawling has recently received a lot of attention. I love that there is more awareness about the importance of crawling, but I hate the amount of anxiety, fear and guilt that I see in parents. Crawling is great for babies, but it is not a guarantee that your baby is going to graduate *cum laude* from university. You need to take some of the pressure off yourself and your baby, and encourage gross motor development through play.

As discussed earlier, the brain uses a 'use it or lose it' system. Your baby needs to form and use certain pathways to keep them. The movement patterns that work in a certain environment will be kept, and those that do not work will be lost. If a baby can use bottom shuffling to move around on a smooth floor, then they won't need to use crawling. If a baby is in baby gear and not on the floor, then they won't need to use crawling and won't do so. It is not uncommon for babies who do not learn to crawl in the first year to never learn to crawl. The 'crawling' pathways have not been used, so they have faded away.

If your baby ends up skipping crawling and going straight to walking, as some babies do, all is not lost. You can still encourage your baby to use a variety of movement patterns and experience a variety of sensorimotor experiences.

Try to expose your older baby (from about 9 months) to different environments that ask for different movement patterns:

1. Clamber over things that are different heights indoors (think cushions, couches) and outdoors (think steps, logs and boulders).
2. Pretend to be an animal like a puppy dog or bunny rabbit on the grass.
3. Practise climbing ladders or exploring low trees.
4. Set up a tunnel or tent to move through.
5. Put things under chairs and tables, and do a treasure hunt.

The benefits of crawling

Let's look at how this movement pattern influences your baby's brain, bones and muscles.

1. **Crawling benefits your baby's brain.** It requires that both hemispheres of the brain work together and integrate the information they receive from the four limbs, the head and the trunk. The right hemisphere receives information from the left side and the left hemisphere receives information from the right side. Each hemisphere is also responsible for feeding instructions back to the opposite side.

   Between the two hemispheres is a thick band called the corpus callosum. The more frequently information 'crosses over' from the right to the left hemisphere and vice versa, the thicker this band grows. This 'thickness' is caused by the rapid growth of nerve cells to support the use of the whole brain.

   As we saw earlier, in the first year of life there is an explosion of new nerve cells that allow your baby to develop all kinds of skills. At the end of the first year of life, there is a massive culling that takes place. Any nerve cells that were not used and any pathways that proved inefficient die out. While this sounds like a bad thing, this death actually promotes coordination and speed as the baby develops a higher-quality operating system with less interference. Your baby's brain gets an upgrade, but in the process it dumps all apps that are hardly ever used.

So, while crawling is a temporary skill, necessary for only a few months of one's life, it is the period when the corpus collosum thickens so that the brain can work in a coordinated way for the many, many years to come.

The brain is greatly altered by crawling – as are the bones and muscles.

2. **Crawling benefits your baby's bones.** Babies don't have the same bony skeleton that you do. Instead, their joints are cartilaginous and form over time, dependent on the forces that influence them. For example, they are born with soft skulls with large holes in them, no wrist bones, open hip joints, no kneecaps, and thin feet with pointy heels.

Muscles that pull on the bone via their ropey tendons will change the shape of the bones, as will the weight of a baby's body. From birth, babies battle against gravity after a blissful, weightless existence. Here is how crawling benefits your baby's skeletal development.

Your baby will gain one wrist bone a year for roughly the first 12 years of their life. In crawling, these bones change shape as your baby puts weight through their hands into the floor. This change helps develop stable wrists that the baby can use for protecting themselves from falling, as well as playing sports, as they grow.

Putting weight through the hand also causes the hand

bones to 'spread out'. You will notice that your baby is developing creases in their palm as they use their hands to support themselves and reach for objects. These arches of the hand allow the hand to fold and hold in various ways that make the hands more useful tools.

As some of your baby's weight is taken through his pelvis during crawling, the previously flat hip joint curves to kiss the neck of the long thigh bone (the femur). This curvature gives the hip joint stability, which the baby needs before attempting to transfer their full weight through their pelvis in independent standing.

3. **Crawling benefits your baby's muscle development.** Spend some time down on your hands and knees and you will soon learn that crawling offers a unique, whole-body workout. The areas that are most notably tired after a few minutes? All of them! That's because crawling strengthens the muscles of the neck, shoulders, back, stomach, hips, legs and arms, contributing specifically to:

   - **Head control.** Crawling calls on the muscles at the back of the neck and back to contract and hold up the head and body against gravity.

   - **Shoulder stability.** Crawling strengthens the muscles between the shoulder blades, pulling the shoulder blades flat onto the back (rather than projecting upwards like a cat's). This change is key to gaining shoulder stability. Shoulder stability protects your baby when they fall. It also allows a baby to take on an upright posture in which the arm is free to act as an arm, rather than a leg that is used to support the body's weight.

- **Pelvic stability.** Crawling changes the muscles of the pelvis and stomach. Before a baby crawls, their bottom will point up and their tummy will sag, causing a severe curve in their lower spine. Crawling tightens up these core muscles. It pulls the bottom out of the air and down towards the floor. Again, this is key for a baby who is destined to stand and requires good pelvic stability to walk, run and kick.

- **Wrist stability.** Crawling develops stable wrist joints, with strong muscles at the back of the forearm (known as wrist extensors). Babies who do not crawl often have poor wrist stability, so they battle to carry a plate or use a bat to hit a ball. This stability is key for more complex fine motor tasks like writing and cutting.

Should my baby be crawling already?

Most babies start crawling in some shape or form between seven and nine months. However, there are many signs you can watch for in the months preceding this milestone to reassure you that your baby is making progress in the days leading up to their first cute crawl video.

- **Wait a minute, you were on your back!?** As terrifying as this can be at first, if you find your baby in a different position from that in which you left them lying in the cot or on the floor, it means your baby is starting to transition. Transitioning is moving from one position to another independently. This means that the muscle groups of their head, shoulders and pelvis are beginning to talk to one another. This is great. Rolling is the first transitional movement. Pushing up from side lying into sitting is also a transitional movement.

- **Why are you moving backwards?!** Strangely enough, most babies start moving backwards rather than forwards. On their tummy, they will push their arms and slide backwards. When leopard crawling, they will make more progress backwards than forwards. And when in puppy position (four-point kneeling), they will rock both forwards and backwards before moving anywhere. This is totally normal, and a great sign that they are experimenting with moving in different ways.

- **Why is your bum in the air?!** Many babies will 'face plant' a few times while trying to work out this crawling gig. Some may even push up into bear walking (a position where the arms and legs are straight), which can make many parents raise an eyebrow. Any progress forwards on hands, feet, or tummy is fantastic, and should be encouraged.

Walking

Walking is the third 'big' gross motor milestone, and happens between 10 and 20 months of age. This makes it the skill with the widest developmental window. Nobody can prepare you for the joy that you experience watching your baby take their first steps.

To get to true, independent walking, babies need to conquer gravity in smaller bits. They need to be able to:

- Pull from sit to stand holding on to furniture (from about eight months)
- Cruise or step from side to side while holding on to furniture (from about eight months)
- Step forward with one or two hands held (from about eight months).

Babies will stand up first in an assisted way, usually held up in standing by their parents. They have a standing reflex, so weight through their heels triggers their entire body to extend or stand up. You can play for short periods with your baby in this standing position. Giving your baby support in standing can give them a taste of what it's like to be truly upright. There is nothing wrong with this – however, your baby will also need time learning to stand unassisted. Once again, this will happen from time on the floor.

The benefits of walking

Walking brings many seen and unseen benefits to your baby.

1. **Walking benefits your baby's brain.** A baby who is walking is using both sides of their body in an asymmetrical pattern. This further strengthens the corpus callosum and the communication between the brain's left and right hemispheres. Walking further alters the brain's visual centre, as it allows a baby to see and make sense of the world at a different height. This is good news for development, but bad news for your tablecloths and neatly packed kitchen drawers.

2. **Walking moulds your baby's bones.** The weight that your baby takes when standing and walking will change their joints, in terms of both their shape and their purpose. Standing helps to close the hip joints and makes the pelvis more stable. This allows for a stable base for the legs to move from. Standing and walking also helps to

shape the ankle joints to create stability and allow reliable weight bearing. Your baby's feet are also shaped at this time. Watch how your baby's once-pointy heels widen and their feet start to develop arches as they move their foot in different ways.

3. **Walking increases your baby's social interaction.** Many cultures view walking as a graduation from helpless baby to curious toddler. A baby who can walk is seen as a real person, and often gets more attention and verbal interaction than a baby who is not walking. Equally, a baby who is walking might also start more conversations, moving towards other kids and adults.

4. **Walking aids digestion.** Mobility improves gut motility. Many babies are said to 'walk away' from reflux, cramps and constipation. As the trunk muscles strengthen and the baby becomes more upright, gravity assists with many of these painful digestive issues.

5. **Walking lets babies go hands-free.** A baby can truly start using their hands once they are walking. Yes, sure, for the first few weeks of walking most babies use their arms to help with balance and to protect themselves during the many stumbles they face. But when the wobbling stops, suddenly your baby has two hands that they can use to wave and blow kisses, to push and pull, to reach and release, to explore and to experiment with all kinds of fun games.

If walking has so many advantages, why do walking rings get such a bad rap?

Walking rings can help babies get upright and zoom around and give parents some hands-free time of their own. The reason why so many families pass their walking rings down through the generations is because babies love them!

Giving a baby a walking ring is like giving an eight-year-old the keys to a car. Neither the kid nor the baby has had the chance to develop the underlying skills necessary to use these devices safely. Can a child drive a car? Yes they can. But should they drive it? I would say no!

Let's look at why developmental specialists hate walking rings so passionately.

There are many wise sayings like, 'You need to learn to walk before you can run,' and 'Everything in its own good time.' The same is true for your baby's syllabus (what they are mastering) in their first year of life. Babies need the time they spend lying horizontally to prepare them for the time they spend walking vertically. There is no benefit to your baby learning to walk 'early' through the use of a walking ring.

Babies who have used walking rings may walk on their toes as they are not used to controlling their pelvis, so they 'fix' themselves upright by using other muscles (like the ones in their arms and neck). This poor form may lead to considerable postural problems later in life.

In addition, a baby who uses a walking ring to learn to walk usually skips crawling altogether. And remember, once your baby is upright they rarely go back to the floor – which means they could miss out on all the bits in between: the dashes that we spoke about earlier. Like all skills we need to develop, a series of steps usually needs to be followed. Picture a tower that is being built brick by brick. One or two missing bricks is really no big deal, but take too many bricks away and the tower will fall.

Sitting and crawling and walking independently are due to the culmination of a series of developmental achievements. These include learning to lift one's head against gravity, learning to use the hands together as well as separately, learning to use the legs together as well as separately, and learning to coordinate pretty complex movement patterns that use all four limbs and both sides of the body.

When they learn to move off the floor, babies gain freedom, but from a low height. Struggle is a critical part of development, so bumps and grazes are essential learning blocks. However, bumps and grazes from a floor position often end a lot more happily than bumps and grazes from an upright position – or worse, an upright, hanging, running position that is the walking ring. Walking rings are renowned for helping babies launch head-first down stairs, and reach up higher to pull appliances off counters. In some countries, such as Canada, walking rings are banned for these reasons.

If you must use a walking ring, please do not leave your baby unsupervised. They will be an incredibly dangerous solo driver. They will have speed, but no control or awareness – a recipe for disaster.

And don't panic: using a walking ring for 15 minutes a day is probably not going to do your baby any harm. It's the babies who are hanging out in their walking ring for two to three hours a day that I am worried about. It is not just the time spent in the walking ring that is the problem – what your baby is missing out on outside the walking ring also concerns me. Too little time outside baby devices can lead to the following outcomes for your baby:

- Walking with a wide, 'cowboy' stance that makes it difficult to run quickly or change direction
- Difficulty understanding their own body schema, resulting in clumsiness – frequently bumping into things that 'have always been there' in the house

242

- Lack of experience in moving off the ground, leading to weak core, arm and shoulder muscles
- A posterior pelvic tilt (sitting on the back of your bottom), making it hard to learn to sit upright in ring time and at the desk.

Remember, practise does not make perfect – it makes permanent. Brain cells that fire together wire together, so choose a safer, slower path to walking and ditch the walking ring.

Are the grandparents begging to buy your late walker something to help them get going? Request a low, wooden wagon filled with wooden blocks. It is a great developmental tool that supports walking too. If you weight it with bricks or books so that it is very heavy and stable, it can offer your baby a slower ride.

And for those who want to know if their baby is late, as the grandparents say, this chart is very useful for determining the range of normal in the first two years. It was first published in a

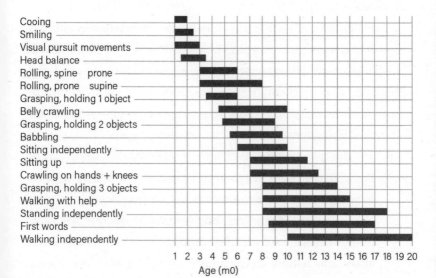

1976 article entitled 'Neurological Development in Infancy', and shows how widely human beings vary. For example, sitting independently can occur anywhere from 6–11 months, crawling from 7–13 months and walking from 10–20 months.

Rather than racing towards gross motor milestones and missing out on all the good stuff that happens in between, you are focusing on these four principles:

1. **Is your baby asking to play?** A baby who wants to play will tell you. As an occupational therapist, I am always comforted when I see a baby 'reaching' out with their eyes attracting adults and children to come and talk, giggle and move with them. This interaction will provide your baby with both the sensory and the motor opportunities they need to develop gross motor skills.

2. **Is your baby curious to explore?** While parents often dismay that their babies are getting into things that they shouldn't, it is this need to explore the environment and discover toys (and plug sockets!) that drives motor development. No one moves without a reason. If your baby is finding plenty of reasons to push into sitting, pull to stand and get up those stairs, there is no way that gravity is going to win.

3. **Can your baby move in a variety of ways?** Want another reason to celebrate? Look at the many ways in which your baby can move. Rather than trying to force crawling, celebrate your baby's reaching out on their tummy, rocking on their knees and sticking their cute butt in the air. All these seemingly unrelated and less useful

movements will become the reason why your baby can get in and out of sitting, crawl in many directions and protect their precious head when they do start walking. The time to worry is if your baby seems stuck in one position and is not making even small progress from week to week and month to month.

4. **Does your baby love movement?** You know you are on to a good thing when your baby just loves moving, with or without your help. Babies who love swinging, dancing, rough-and-tumbling, or frolicking in the pool are laying a solid gross motor foundation that will benefit them long after the first two years. They are likely to go on to become healthy and active children and adults, with a wide variety of interests and abilities.

Answering these four questions is a better way of gauging whether something is going right or wrong in your baby's gross motor development than using months and milestones, which can be deceiving – and, for some babies, can even delay the intervention they need. The goal is not to race through skill acquisition and be walking by one, but rather to allow your child to discover and enjoy a wonderfully rich world of movement.

River the mattress baby's story

River was a baby born to a warm and loving family. As the first grandchild, there was no shortage of love. He spent most of his day entertained in the arms of adults – his nanny, parents and grandparents adored him, as they should.

Nobody liked to see River unhappy, so he was seldom put down on the floor or left in his cot to explore on his own.

At 10 months old, he was happy to sit if placed upright in a soft spot with access to snacks and entertainment. River loved his padded high chair, the car seat and the couch.

His parents sought my help as they were starting to worry. His first birthday was approaching and he could barely move. He was not rolling, could not get in or out of sitting and cried if held in standing. He hated any weight through his hands or feet, and disliked being moved out of his ring-sitting position. He would cry if he wanted a toy that was out of his reach, rather than making a plan to get to it.

In my practice, I refer to babies like River as 'mattress' babies. They are so loved and protected that they never experience any failure, and are therefore delayed in their learning. They are protected by padding – in their cot, in the car seat and in their loving family's arms. They have experienced neither struggle nor the pain of not succeeding. They are often heavy babies, as they are being fed but are not using much energy to move.

River needed to be introduced to the world beyond the mattress where, if you did not control your body, you could get hurt. This was unacceptable news to his mother, who imagined him bashing his head on the tiles and grazing his knees on the bricks.

I explained that all he needed was a little more firmness.

- A wooden box would be a better alternative to his padded highchair.
- Sitting with his feet touching the solid floor when on someone's lap would be better than sitting on a lap with his feet dangling in space.
- Lying on a firm mat would be better than lying on a soft bed or couch.

Getting some feedback from these solid surfaces would be the only way in which River could change what he was doing – small amounts of pain and small tastes of failure make us all stronger as we work harder to try, try and try again, eventually to conquer.

During therapy, I suggested to his mother that he try lying on her chest to start. Unused to this position, he banged his forehead on her sternum and let out a big wail. It was too much for her. She was up and out of my room; she could not bear to see him unhappy.

One of the greatest challenges of parenting is this: knowing when to remove our children from a difficult situation and offer them comfort, and knowing when to keep them in an uncomfortable position, supporting them as they learn outside their comfort zones.

At the practice, I do not work through the tears. I have a no-cry policy and respect a baby's cues. I know there are enough positions, games and strategies that can be used without babies or young children needing to cry. However, I am also aware that a parent's role is not only to protect, but also to prepare. Yes, we must protect our children from the hard, cold world, but we must also prepare them to live there.

Each parent will need to dance between protecting and preparing as time goes on. But if your baby seems 'stuck', you may need to consider a new approach.

Pumi and Thumi's story

The term 'Siamese twins' comes from the first pair of famous conjoined twins, Chang and Eng Bunker, who were from Siam, China. These brothers were joined from shoulder to hip and lived in the 1800s. It is not often in your life that you see Siamese twins, let alone get to watch them be separated.

But two babies I worked with were. Twin sisters, Pumi and Thumi, were joined from their chest bones to their belly buttons. They had their own set of arms and legs but sat facing each other, sharing a tummy. They each had their own heart but shared a heart sac. They each had a stomach but shared a liver. They each had one kidney but luckily had their own intestines. Separation was possible under the care of the right surgical team.

Until they were old enough to undergo separation surgery, Pumi and Thumi lived in one cot in the hospital at which I worked. They were 18 months old when they underwent surgery and found themselves physically apart from each other, in their own cots, for the first time. Something was wrong after the surgery. Neither girl could settle to sleep. Their vitals were not good. They seemed distressed, despite the pain medication they were receiving.

The anaesthetist and I decided to reunite them in one cot to see if being 'back together' would help. It did! It took a while for their extensive wounds to heal, but while they were recovering they chose to lie tummy to tummy, as they had done prior to surgery.

There were concerns, of course. What if one got an infection and gave it to the other? What if one kicked or scratched the other's skin grafts? Luckily, the toddlers treated each other as gently as they had before separation.

Unsurprisingly, once they entered the rehabilitation phase they hated tummy time. They were not used to the feeling of a hard surface under them. They had always had their twin's soft body under their chest. It was fascinating to watch them discover this 'new' extra side of their body as time went on. They learnt to roll and move and sit up. They had regular physiotherapy and occupational therapy, and they did go on to crawl – but very briefly. Two-year-olds do not want to be down on the ground practising crawling. They want to be up walking and engaging at the level of all their friends.

Yes, they missed out on months of tummy time and crawling, but they went on to be toddlers who could run and squat and play.

Sometimes, babies do not have an ideal start, like Pumi and Thumi. Perhaps your baby has not had an easy time learning to move against gravity. Do not give up. There are many things you can do to support your baby's learning to use their whole body to move, both now and later. Focus on what your baby can do and try to give them a chance to do it more and more. As their confidence to move grows, you can start introducing new activities.

Many babies with special needs will never develop 'typical' movements, but they may go on to enjoy movement in whatever form they can. Experiencing a variety of ways to move should be the goal for all babies, no matter how they start their life.

REALITY 9: Your baby needs more than tummy time to develop good postural control

- The Unicorn Baby loves to play on their tummy. They are happy to be left for 20 minutes to play alone with their toys. Your baby may hate being left on the floor. And that's okay.
- To learn, babies need to feel safe as much as they need to play in a variety of positions to develop a wide variety of movements.
- Do not force your baby to endure tummy time on the floor. Find an alternate position that suits them.

- Try to avoid putting your baby in devices with only one position, such as baby seats and walking rings.
- There are many things you can do to support your baby's learning to use their whole body to move – both now and later. Learning is a lifelong process.

Learning is a lifelong process

Signs that you are busting Myth 9

✔ Your baby is asking to play.

✔ Your baby is curious to explore people and everyday objects. They love experiencing new sensorimotor activities.

✔ Your baby is happy in a variety of positions; firstly, horizontally and later, vertically.

✔ Your baby loves moving around both in your arms and on surfaces.

Myth 10
Technology gives you and your baby an advantage

The Unicorn Baby is a well-recorded baby. Their feeds, naps and milestones are recorded daily on various apps and platforms. This data helps their high-tech parents make decisions. If the app says their baby needs more sleep, they get more sleep. If the app says they are feeding too often, feeds are spaced and paced. If the app says they need that toy now, it is ordered online and delivered to their door. The Unicorn Baby, like their parents, is well-versed in tech. They know how to pop bubbles and match shapes on an iPad screen. They are comforted by FaceTiming their mom at work. They are learning Mandarin thanks to YouTube and will surely be coding by age five.

We are the first generation of parents in history to be co-parenting with technology. Let that sink in. We are the first participants in this great experiment that is titled 'the impact of technology on babies and their parents'. Research has followed children from birth to age five. What it has shown is that screen time has had a negative effect on babies and preschoolers. When a child is younger than three years old, time spent on devices has no educational or developmental benefit. Your baby is not going to be at an advantage because they have a puzzle app.

More worrying is that time spent on devices is linked to:

1. Physical inactivity that leads to childhood obesity
2. Problems with attention and aggression in the preschool years
3. Development of myopia or short-sightedness by age five
4. More chance of developing language difficulties.

We know a little about the effect on our babies and young kids, but we know even less about the long-term effect that technology will have on our families and society at large.

It is only in the past five to ten years that we have begun raising our babies as per the website or app's instructions, so we really do not know if we are better or worse off than the generations who went before us. What drives parents to use technology is the idea that technology gives them an advantage. The myth is this: if you use technology, it will tell you exactly what to do. It will make parenting easier. It will take away the need to deliberate or worry.

I have observed a few worrying trends when it comes to co-parenting with technology:

1. **Connecting to a device means you are disconnecting from your baby.** Babies are born with an underdeveloped visual system. It is dark inside the womb, so birth is the start of a baby being able to see. A baby needs to learn to control the movements of each eye and to use the eyes together as a team – to see near and far, as well as to look across a space.

   When a baby is born, their eyes can focus at about 12–30 cm. This is the perfect distance for two things: seeing their mother's face and spotting the nipple to feed. It is the responsibility of the visual cortex (the area of the brain dedicated to vision and visual perception) to talk to other areas of the brain so that visual learning can occur. For example, when your baby sees you smile and experiences joy, a connection will be made between the visual cortex (understanding what is seen), the limbic system (where emotions come from) and the hippocampus (where memories are stored). If a baby is not seeing your face, this connection will be less developed.

   Many new parents will try to record feeds and poops and naps on an app. This can help to alleviate any fears and give you great data to show anyone interested, such as nurses, your paediatrician, or your high-school bestie. The downside, however, is that this can also interrupt the beautiful process of synchronisation or attunement that should be happening daily between you and your baby.

   Attunement is when you and your baby get to know each other. It is a time of subtle change and accommodation that add up to things just working. As you know by now, babies are changing all the time, so you need to re-synch regularly. It is how you stay connected. For this to happen (and keep happening), you need to be face to face or eye to eye often.

Unfortunately, because apps are usually located on smart devices, it will mean that once you pick up your device to log some data onto the app *boom* there is everything else in the world that could distract you from your baby. From to-do lists to work e-mails, from the latest hit to the replies on your last gorgeous post on the 'gram. It is so hard to get on and get off without going down that rabbit hole. Unfortunately for many babies, this means they have a device between them and their parent. And there is often a very hostile reaction if the baby dares to grab or knock the device.

What your baby learns is that there is this third 'person' in the relationship. The device is enthralling, a priority in everyone's lives. A pattern of interaction with technology is established. Baby does what they have seen done before – they give more of their attention to screens and less to people.

2. **Babies are learning to play with devices rather than with people or toys.** Parents notice that their babies are interested in their devices. So, to keep the peace, they either add some child-friendly content to their device or purchase their baby their very own device. Usually, this device is designed to survive all manner of thrills and spills. It can be easily wiped should baby drool. It bounces when dropped. And it can – and does – go along everywhere.

Unfortunately, the more time your baby spends staring at a flat screen, the less opportunity they have to develop eye movements – to look both near and far and across to find an object. Your baby's visual world has become super-interesting, but has been reduced to an area of 30 cm × 20 cm.

This further reduces the inner drive to move to get to the next interesting person or toy. Babies move only because there is a reason to move. A baby with onboard entertainment is unlikely to move and develop their mobility skills.

Your baby also has less opportunity to explore what they see with their hands and mouth. Seeing a leaf falling on a screen is interesting, but it does not allow you to reach out and grab the leaf or bring it to your mouth. This creates a disconnect between the eyes, hands and mouth, organs which should be in almost constant communication while a baby is learning to eat, speak and play.

This further negatively impacts the variety of hand positions or grasps that your baby can use. Playing with another person's fingers or grasping a naartjie asks a baby to do very different hand movements than palming a screen does. A human hand should have well-developed arches and move in many different planes of movement, however, these only develop when and if they are needed. A baby who is interacting with a screen only needs to swipe, palm and point. Their hands only need to be flat and one-dimensional.

Lastly, and most importantly, a baby who is interacting with a screen is not interacting with people. The first year is all about learning to communicate with others. The more your baby sees facial expressions and hears spoken language from a three-dimensional face and mouth, the more clues your baby will have to use to put together their own sounds and sentences.

Screens are so enticing because i) they are entertaining and ii) they ask so little of us. It is hard for a baby to move away from a screen where there was visual complexity with moving objects, millions of colours and quick transitions between images back to the real world where life is slower and things take longer to come to you.

Screens train babies to expect that life will be easy and fun. Unfortunately, a baby's two greatest tasks, which are growth and learning, cannot always be easy and fun. Babies need to develop both motivation ('I will try this') and perseverance ('I will try this again') in order to become lifelong learners.

3. **Parents are using technology to distract during key learning moments.** I feel overwhelmed when parents tell me that they can only feed their baby if the TV or iPad is on. Why do I feel so hopeless? It is because I know that if

a baby is only eating when distracted then something is going wrong within their experience of feeding.

If a baby has to be distracted to eat, then they are clearly not an active participant in the meal and are clearly not enjoying the meal provided. It is an overwhelming scenario, as I am well aware that the family needs to change before the baby's eating habits can.

Using technology to distract during key learning moments is also evident when visiting public spaces. I have seen babies given devices in the car on their way home from the clinic, in the shopping trolley at the supermarket, in the pram on the walk home and at the table at family restaurants. There is no interaction with the baby unless something goes wrong. Then there is a distressed wail until the screen is reconfigured.

In this way, it is not what they are getting from the screen that is the problem but what they are missing out on while glued to it. Outings should give your baby lots of experiences: they should be listening to your words as you tell them about where you are going and what is happening; they should be seeing lots of new and familiar things; and they should be learning to wait – that things take time, and that in life you will not be entertained all the time.

I also see it during play dates. Play dates are arranged to teach positive social interaction – but often, at the moment that the play becomes too messy or the babies start poking at one another's eyes – the screen is quickly whipped out and used as a distraction. Yes, it prevents those awkward moments where you have to teach your baby, 'We don't bite friends,' but it also prevents social learning. Babies and kids need to learn how to behave socially. It is not an automatic skill. Often, it is at the point where the most learning was about to happen that kids are distracted by the lure of a screen.

The reality is that, as new parents, you will need to learn to trust what you experience in the real world with your baby more than what technology might tell you. You will also have to model to your baby how to interact wisely with technology. The recommendation for babies in the first year of life is no screen time whatsoever. You may need to think carefully how you can help your family stick to this, especially if you add more babies to the family.

My recommendations to parents are these:

- **Don't buy your baby a device.** If it is not there, it is not an option – and so it is much easier to find something else to play with.
- **Get off your device when you can.** Try to model a healthy relationship with screens. You may need to get a grip on your screen time addiction before you can help your baby get a grip on theirs.
- **Rotate your baby's toys.** Use three large storage boxes. Divide your baby's toys, or the safe and interesting objects you have approved for your baby to play with, between these three boxes. Every week or two, rotate the boxes so that your baby gets exposed

to some novel items. A toy could be anything from a beaded necklace to a sealed plastic bottle filled with some macaroni. An interesting object could be a leaf, a baby shoe, or a wooden spoon.

- **Make a play pack.** When you go out, take a bag with a few favourites and a few novel items along with you. Babies love things that move. My go-to items would be a ball, a car, train, or tractor with moving wheels, a beaded necklace, a few wooden blocks, some ribbon, a cork and a plastic mirror. Your baby can interact with these objects if you need to wait in a queue or if a trip takes longer than expected.

- **Use sound.** If you need to distract your baby, rather use an auditory stimulus like a song. It is corny, but singing a song can help your baby understand and anticipate what is coming next. You can make up songs as you go or use some golden oldies like the 'pack away' song. Learning to listen to sounds is a great skill. There are also many audiobooks that you can listen to whilst looking at a real book. This is a better alternative to a visual reading app. Download kid-friendly songs (that you don't completely hate) and enjoy using these as the soundtrack to your early days together.

My story: Paying attention to your baby

I have always wanted to be a present mother, but wanting to be present is not the same as being present. Over the past nine years my children have wrestled against the pull of my work e-mails, our household chores and the many notifications that pop up on my social media accounts.

I have seen first hand how my children's behaviour deteriorates when I am functioning in a continual state of distraction. My kids whine, fight and froth until I realise that what I am lacking in that moment, they are lacking too . . . attention.

Deciding to turn off the screens in my home and put my to-do list on ice for fifteen minutes is often all that is needed to restore happiness in the home. Here are five small habits you can pick up to help you and your little one learn to attend to one task at a time.

1. **Model focused attention.** Living in this age of distraction has done little to assist our children to acquire attention skills. Attention can be visual (think reading a book) or auditory (think following instructions). It can be a flicker, or it can be a marathon. However, without attention, there can be no learning.

   Focused attention starts at birth. Mother and babe lock eyes, mama smiles, babe takes it all in. It's a beautiful moment and should be just the beginning of many necessary moments of eye contact. Eye contact is the start of bonding, building trust and reading non-verbal cues. It needs to exist long before there is joint attention – when mother and babe share an experience together, like singing a song, looking at a picture book or staring up at a dancing leaf. Joint attention is the first step towards developing long-term attention skills. The good news is that, in the second half of the first year, it's as simple as taking turns playing hide-and-seek and pointing out cool things that you find along your way.

A full-term newborn mimics facial expressions (go ahead and stick your tongue out and see what your baby does). The downside of this amazing 'copycat' ability is that, as time goes on, your baby will continue to imitate you. If you are able to model sustained attention and stay focused on a task, your baby stands a better chance of finishing tasks too.

Model turning off devices and having intentional eye-to-eye moments at the dinner table and at bedtime. Keep track of how long your baby can look at pictures or listen to stories for, and you should notice a general upward trend. As your baby gets bigger, they should be able to listen and look for longer.

2. **Embrace boredom.** Allowing your child to use a familiar toy in a new way promotes attention, creativity and problem-solving. As you know, toys that offer many types of play are my favourite as they let the child take the lead, rather than prescribing the interaction. For example, a stick can be a chew toy, a hammer or a magic wand... your child chooses the track. My kids have loved playing with cardboard boxes at every age. Give them time to see how they can turn a box into a cave, a chair and a castle.

3. **Limit the options.** To help prevent your child from flitting between toys, limit the number of toys they can access. A baby with too many options may lack the impulse control necessary to fully explore with one toy before moving on to the next. The amount and variety of screen time to which babies are exposed can also limit their ability to focus on less 'exciting' play, so try to limit the amount of time they spend passively staring at a screen.

Look carefully at the pace and content of the shows to which your kids are exposed. A short, slow-moving, very simple show where real people sing one or two songs will be less exciting and stimulating than putting on a YouTube channel that has all kinds of visual effects and cartoon characters zooming around. Beware of channels and games that are endless and whose next episode loads automatically. Being able to watch television or play a game on the iPad for a really long time is not the same as being able to play with your cars for an hour. Unfortunately, the length of time for which they can sit still and watch a screen is not an accurate measure of your child's attention skills.

4. **Check your expectations.** At the practice, I use a child's age as a guide to how long to spend doing each difficult activity. A rough guide for parents is that a one year old should focus for one minute before moving to another task, a two year old two minutes, and so on. If you would like your three year old to sit still and colour in for 15 minutes, it may be your expectation that's off and not your child's ability to concentrate. Some children do exceed these guidelines, and this is wonderful, but if yours doesn't build LEGO for an hour it doesn't mean something is wrong. In fact, it is actually a sign of healthy development if a child is intensely curious and seeks to explore their environment fully.

5. **Pay attention during feeding.** The first few days of a child's life are dedicated to establishing feeding. Whether you feed via breast or bottle, try to feed in a quieter space where your baby can start understanding that we

need to attend while we are eating. Healthy eating allows the child to be active and explore the food. Allow lots of breaks for communication . . . chat about the food, and how it tastes and smells and feels. The goal is to raise a kid who can sit around a table and enjoy a meal face to face. Babies who eat in front of the TV are robbed of this training.

Rudy and Jack's story

I met Rudy first. He was four years old and accompanied by his elderly grandparents. They were in my waiting room and Rudy was eyeballing a bright-orange kiddie's tablet. He seemed stuck. Literally: his hands and eyes were glued to the device.

His grandparents had just returned from Canada from where they had rescued the two boys from their well-meaning parents. Both parents were professionals, working and studying towards postgraduate qualifications. It snowed for most of the year, so the boys had been permitted to stream endlessly while their parents tried their best to study for their exams.

It had been two years since the grandparents had seen the boys, and what they had found had horrified them. At the age of four, Rudy could not walk the three blocks to his preschool. He was still pushed in a pram – clutching his device, of course. His younger brother Jack, at age two, was not making eye contact or any attempt at verbal communication. The grandparents wanted to know if these boys were perhaps developmentally delayed. They had never seen little boys so unwilling to play and explore.

I assessed Rudy first, and the results were sad indeed. He was globally developmentally delayed by more than two years. Convinced that his little brother Jack could not be as bad, I suggested that I assess him too to see where intervention could overlap for them both.

I was shocked to find that they shared many common difficulties. They had a hunched-over grandpa posture from leaning over devices; they both swiped with their whole hand at everyday objects such as a pencil; despite doing 100-piece puzzles on their devices, neither could hold or put together a three-, four-, or five-piece puzzle in real life; they could not hold a back-and-forth conversation, and they could not eat anything if they were not watching. Jack could not even hold a bottle, cup or spoon to feed himself. And neither showed any awareness of needing the toilet. They were both still in nappies.

I struggled to believe that all of this could be from just too much screen time and too little physical activity. We all agreed to one-on-one therapy with each boy separately, and then some combined sessions. Could these boys actually learn to interact? I was deeply concerned, but encouraged by their grandparents' willingness to be their primary carers for one year. They committed fully to the therapy process, which at times felt daunting as I was unsure whether they could start behaving differently.

At the next appointment I was amazed to hear that they had decided to go screen-free at home. They were so disturbed by the boys' dependency on their devices that they had gone cold turkey. The whole household. Even grandpa was willing to miss out on the cricket. I was amazed that they had all survived the trauma.

Therapy focused on sensorimotor experiences for both Rudy and Jack. They were given the chance to move, and to feel what they hadn't felt. It was scary for them. It was slow going, but

I started to see progress. Their little hands became less sensitive and less weak; their bodies became a little stronger and able to do more than they had thought they could; they started taking turns at rolling a ball and winning at games; they could speak in three- to five-word sentences and started smiling! The developmental gaps were getting narrower.

Despite the progress, there were two things that persisted. Firstly, both struggled to sustain eye contact appropriately during an interaction. Their heads and eyes felt stuck in that tech-neck downward glance position. If you got under their gaze, eye contact could happen, but they did not look around to initiate it. Secondly, they spoke more but their speech had a peculiar accent and rhythm. They spoke like an American robot rather than using their parents and grandparent's distinctive South African accent. It was clear that the only place they would have heard this accent was during screen time.

I learnt that some habits can be broken, and others seem to persist. After that year, the boys were reunited with their parents. Now that they are older, I am not sure how they are doing or whether they have experienced any other developmental problems. It was fascinating to see how much the ordinary and everyday things that we do can shape who we become.

REALITY 10: You need to learn to trust yourself rather than technology

- You and your baby need to spend more time together and less time on your devices.
- The Unicorn Baby is technology literate. They have their own device and know how to use it. It goes everywhere with them, providing them with stimulation. Parents of a Unicorn Baby are dedicated to using parenting apps diligently and logging all events. They think this gives them a parenting 'advantage' as they know everything about their baby and can follow the app's advice.
- But we are the first generation co-parenting with technology. We do not know how this experiment is going to turn out. As a new parent of a Non-Unicorn Baby, you will do well to slowly learn to trust yourself more than technology.
- Devices are problematic for three reasons:
  1. Connecting to a device means that you are disconnecting from your baby.
  2. Babies are learning to play with devices rather than with people or toys.
  3. Parents are using technology to distract during key learning moments.
- If you want your baby to pay attention, you need to pay attention to your baby.

Signs that you are busting Myth 10

✔ You have spent more time getting to know your baby than researching babies on your phone.

✔ You and your baby have synchronised – you watch for their cues rather than instructions from an app.

✔ Your baby likes to play with people.

✔ Your baby likes to play with a variety of toys.

✔ Your baby can eat without watching a screen.

✔ Your baby can go to the park, drive in a car and go to a play date without a device coming along.

✔ You are learning to trust yourself more than technology.

Conclusion

As we have explored each myth, I trust that you have found a few interesting bits of information and gathered some practical tips along the way. It really helps to explore these myths with your partner so that you can learn and plan together, updating your road maps together.

Don't be surprised if you have different opinions. You may have fundamentally different personalities and have had different up-bringings, and this will influence how you choose to parent your baby. Don't worry about this. Variety is wonderful! It is okay to agree to disagree on some things.

Once the two of you have formulated a general plan, I suggest that you find a time to chat through what you have learnt and how you would like to go ahead with your baby's care team – the people who are helping you raise your baby. This may be a granny, nanny or day mother.

Get the conversation started. You don't have to be locked in to one rigid plan, but make your wishes known – and, even better, hear from those who may have gone before you and raised a baby or two already. Make sure it is a two-way conversation rather than a download. Communicating well about issues that affect your baby is key to keeping your baby, and the village that will help you raise them, happy.

As you take some time to process the information in this book, I hope you will find a way that works for you and your family and will be able to let go of the pressure you have been feeling to 'get it right'. You will probably need to let go more than once as you navigate parenting.

It's okay to do things differently from your peers. It was difficult for me to accept that some of what I had been taught as an occupational therapist did not work for all babies – including mine. I had to look carefully at my 'baby toolkit' and start to use the things that worked, rather than the things I thought should work. Remember, comparison is the thief of all joy; what works for someone else's family may not work for yours.

If you are learning more about your baby each day, if you are taking care of yourself, if you are trying to stay connected to your baby despite the challenges of parenthood, then you are succeeding. There is no such thing as a perfect baby; equally, there is no such thing as the perfect parents or perfect family.

Parenting is hard work. As a proud Parent of Non-Unicorn Babies (PONUB), I will tell you that the magic and beauty is in the 'otherness'. The otherness teaches. It surprises, and can make you brave and strong. The 'otherness' also helps you find your tribe: the pack of parents who have your back and accept your baby, quirks and all. Many lifelong friendships will be born in the trenches of parenthood. Pretending that your journey is all rainbows and glitter may rob you of finding this support.

But who knows, perhaps you are or will be one of the lucky ones and your baby will pee pure gold and poop rainbows. This would mean that you are, or could be, the proud parents of a Unicorn Baby! If that is the case, then me and all the other PONUBs would prefer you kept this to yourself.

We'll be happy to chat once things get easier in, say, 25 years' time? For the parenting road is a long and bumpy one, but also one hell of an adventure.

Sources

Introduction

Peck, S. (1978). *The Road Less Traveled: A New Psychology of Love, Traditional Values and Spiritual Growth*. New, York, NY: Simon and Schuster.

Myth 1: Babies are all the same

Hadders-Algra, M. (2018). Early brain development: Starring the subplate. *Neuroscience and Biobehavioral Reviews* 92: 276–290.

Super, C. (1976). Environmental effects on motor development: The case of 'African infant precocity'. *Developmental Medicine & Child Neurology* 18(5): 561–567.

Ashbury, K. & Plomin, R. (2013). *G is for Genes: The Impact of Genetics on Education and Achievement*. Hoboken, NJ: Wiley-Blackwell.

Hadders-Algra, M. (2017). Neural substrate and clinical significance of general movements: An update. *Developmental Medicine & Child Neurology* 60(1): 39–46.

Kelly, Y., Sacker, A., Schoon, I. & Nazroo, J. (2006). Ethnic differences in achievement of developmental milestones by 9 months of age: The Millennium Cohort Study. *Developmental Medicine & Child Neurology* 48(10): 825–830.

Bergman, N.J. (2014). The neuroscience of birth and the case for Zero Separation. *Curationis* 37(2).

Twins Early Development Study (TEDS). (ongoing).

Lynn, R. (1988). The intelligence of Japanese children. In *Educational Achievement in Japan: Studies in Social Revaluation*. London: Palgrave Macmillan.

Myth 2: A baby does not have to change your life

Moore, E.R., Hepworth, J.T. & Bergman, N. (2003). Early skin-to-skin contact for mothers and their healthy newborn infants. *Cochrane Database of Systematic Reviews* 2003(2), Art. no. CD003519.

Raylene, P. (2013). The Sacred Hour: Uninterrupted skin-to-skin contact immediately after birth. *Newborn and Infant Nursing Reviews* 13(2): 67–72.

Myth 3: You need to get your baby into the perfect routine

Champagne, F.A., Francis, D.D., Mar, A. & Meaney, M.J. (2003). Variations in maternal care in the rat as a mediating influence for the effects of environment on development. *Physiology & Behavior* 79(3):359–371.

Perry, B.D.(2002). Childhood experience and the expression of genetic potential: What childhood neglect tells us about nature and nurture. *Brain and Mind* 3: 79–100.

Mantymaa, M., Luoma, I., Latva, R., Salmelin,R.J. & Tamminen, T. (2015). Shared pleasure in early mother-infant interactions: Predicting lower levels of emotional and behavioural problems in the child and protecting against the influence of parental psychopathology. *Infant Mental Health Journal* 36(2): 223–237.

Winston R. & Chicot, R. (2016). The importance of early bonding on the long-term mental health and resilience of children. *London Journal of Primary Care* 8(1): 12–14.

Myth 4: Breastfeeding comes naturally

UNICEF. (2018). *Breastfeeding: A Mother's Gift, for Every Child*. New York, NY: UNICEF.

Cobb, M.A. & Chiu, S.-H. (2012). Breastfeeding frequency during the first

24 hours of life for the normal newborn. *Journal of Obstetric, Gynecologic, & Neonatal Nursing* 41: S146.

Giannì, M.L. et al. (2020). Exploring the Emotional Breastfeeding Experience of First-Time Mothers: Implications for Healthcare Support. *Frontiers of Pediatrics* 7(8): 199.

Mohrbacher, N. (2010). *Breastfeeding Answers Made Simple: A Guide for Helping Mothers*. Amarillo, TX: Hale.

Watt, J. & Mead, J. (2013). What paediatricians need to know about breastfeeding. *Paediatrics and Child Health* 23(8): 362–366.

Myth 5: You should only feed your baby every four hours

World Health Organization. (2003). *Global Strategy for Infant and Young Child Feeding*. Geneva: World Health Organization.

World Health Organization. (2017). *Guideline: Protecting, Promoting and Supporting Breastfeeding in Facilities Providing Maternity and Newborn Services*. Geneva: World Health Organization.

Hodges, E., Wasser, H., Colgan, B. & Bentley, M. (2016). Development of feeding cues during infancy and toddlerhood. *MCN: The American Journal of Maternal/Child Nursing* 41(4): 244–251.

Satter, E. (2015). Division of Responsibility in Feeding. Madison, WI: The Ellyn Satter Institute.

World Health Organization. (1989). Protecting, promoting and supporting breast-feeding: the special role of maternity services. A joint WHO/UNICEF statement. Geneva: World Health Organization.

Ierodiakonou, D., Garcia-Larsen, V. & Logan, A. (2016). Timing of allergenic food introduction to the infant diet and risk of allergic or autoimmune disease: a systematic review and meta-analysis. *The Journal of the American Medical Association* 316(11): 1181–1192.

Myth 6: You must teach your baby to sleep through the night

Gettler, L.T. & McKenna, J.J. (2011). Evolutionary perspectives on mother–infant sleep proximity and breastfeeding in a laboratory setting. *American Journal of Physical Anthropology* 144(3): 454–462.

Brescianini, S. et al. (2011). Genetic and environmental factors shape infant sleep patterns: A study of 18-month-old twins. *American Journal of Pediatrics* 127(5): e1296-302.

Dionne, G. et al. (2011). Associations between sleep-wake consolidation and language development in early childhood: A longitudinal twin study. *Sleep* 34(8): 987–995.

Blumberg, M.S., Gall, A.J. & Todd, W.D. (2014). The development of sleep–wake rhythms and the search for elemental circuits in the infant brain. *Behavioral Neuroscience* 128(3): 250–263.

Feldman, R. et al. (2013). Parental oxytocin and early caregiving jointly shape children's oxytocin response and social reciprocity. *Neuropsychopharmacology* 38(7): 1154–1162.

McKenna, J.J. (2014). Night waking among breastfeeding mothers and infants: Conflict, congruence or both? *Evolution, Medicine, and Public Health* 2014(1): 40–47.

Mindell, J.A. (2005). *Sleeping Through the Night: How Infants, Toddlers, and Their Parents Can Get a Good Night's Sleep*. New York, NY: William Morrow Paperbacks.

Wiessinger, D., West, D., Smith, L.J. & Pitman, T. (2014). *Sweet Sleep: Nighttime and Naptime Strategies for the Breastfeeding Family*. Raleigh, NC: La Leche League International.

DST-NRF Centre of Excellence in Human Development. (2018). South African 24-hour Movement Guidelines for Birth to Five Years: A healthy 24 Hour Day. DST-NRF Centre of Excellence in Human Development, University of Witwatersrand.

Myth 7: Your baby grows and develops every day

Lawrence, R A. & Lawrence, R.M. (2016). *Breastfeeding: A Guide for the Medical Profession* (8th edition). Philadelphia, PA: Elsevier.

Kent, J.C., Prime, D.K. & Garbin, C.P. (2012). Principles for maintaining or increasing breast milk production. *Journal of Obstetric, Gynecologic, & Neonatal Nursing* 41: 114–121.

American Academy of Family Physicians (AAFP). (2018). Breastfeeding:, Family Physicians Supporting (Position Paper). Available at https://www.aafp.org/about/policies/all/breastfeeding-support.html (accessed 17 January 2018).

Mulder, P.J., Johnson, T.S. & Baker, L.C. (2010). Excessive weight loss in breastfed infants during the postpartum hospitalization. *Journal of Obstetric, Gynecologic, and Neonatal Nursing* 39:15–26.

Namakin, K., Sharifzadeh, G.R., Zardast, M., Khoshmohabbat, Z. & Saboori, M. (2014). Comparison of the WHO Child Growth Standards with the NCHS for Estimation of Malnutrition in Birjand-Iran. *International Journal of Preventive Medicine* 5(5): 653–657.

Wiessinger, D., West, D. & Pitman, T. (2010). *The Womanly Art of Breastfeeding* (8th edition). New York, NY: Ballantine Books.

Raju, T.N.K. (2011). Breastfeeding is a dynamic biological process – not simply a meal at the breast. *Breastfeeding Medicine* 6(5): 257–259.

Brown, A. & Harries, V. (2015). Infant sleep and night feeding patterns during later infancy: Association with breastfeeding frequency, daytime complementary food intake, and infant weight. *Breastfeeding Medicine* 10(5): 246–252.

Myth 8: Your baby needs specialised stimulation classes and educational toys to thrive

Franzsen, D. & Visser, M. (2010). The association of an omitted crawling milestone with pencil grasp and control in five- and six-year-old children. *South African Journal of Occupational Therapy* 40(2): 20.

Nichols, D. (2005). Development of postural control. In J. Case-Smith (ed.), *Occupational Therapy for Children* (5th edition). St. Louis, MO: Elsevier Mosby, p. 279.

Ayres, A.J. (2005). *Sensory Integration and the Child: Understanding Hidden Sensory Challenges* (25th anniversary edition). Los Angeles, CA: Western Psychological Services, p. 57.

Hadders-Algra, M. (2005). Development of postural control during the first 18 months of life. *Neural Plasticity* 12(2–3): 99–108.

Touwen, B.C.L. (1976). Neurological development in infancy. *Clinics in Developmental Medicine* 58. London: Heinemann Medical Books.

Begus, K., Gliga, T. & Southgate, V. (2014). Infants learn what they want to learn: Responding to infant pointing leads to superior learning. *PLoS ONE* 9(10).

Sumner, G. & Spietz, A. (1994). *NCAST Caregiver/Parent-Child Interaction Teaching Manual*. Seattle, WA: NCAST Publications, University of Washington, School of Nursing.

Stagnitti, K. & Unsworth, C. (2000). The importance of pretend play in child development: An occupational therapy perspective. *British Journal of Occupational Therapy* 63(3): 121–127.

Myth 9: Your baby must do tummy time for 20 minutes every day

American Academy of Pediatrics, Task Force on Infant Sleep Position and Sudden Infant Death Syndrome. (2000). Changing concepts of sudden infant death syndrome: Implications for infant sleeping environment and sleep position. *Pediatrics* 105(3): 650–656.

Kahn, A. et al. Sudden infant deaths: Stress, arousal and SIDS. *Early Human Development* 2003: 75 Suppl:S147–S166.

Majnemer, A. & Barr, R.G. (2005). Influence of supine sleep positioning on early motor milestone acquisition. *Developmental Medicine & Child Neurology* 47(6): 370–376.

Carmeli, E., Marmur, R., Cohen, A. & Tirosh, E. (2009). Preferred sleep position and gross motor achievement in early infancy. *European Journal of Pediatrics* 168(6): 711–715.

Davis, B.E., Moon, R.Y., Sachs, H.C. & Ottolini, M.C. (1998). Effects of sleep position on infant motor development. *Pediatrics* 102(5): 1135–1140.

Feijen, M., Franssen, B., Vincken, N. & Van der Hulst, R.R. (2015). Prevalence and consequences of positional plagiocephaly and brachycephaly. *Journal of Craniofacial Surgery* 26(8): e770–e773.

Pin, T., Eldridge, B. & Galea, M.P. (2007). A review of the effects of sleep position, play position, and equipment use on motor development in infants. *Developmental Medicine & Child Neurology* 49(11): 858–867.

Salls, J.S., Silverman, L.N. & Gatty, C.M. (2002). The relationship of infant sleep and play positioning to motor milestone achievement. *American Journal of Occupational Therapy* 56(5): 577–580.

Myth 10: Technology gives you and your baby an advantage

Yang, G.Y. et al. (2020). Associations between screen exposure in early life and myopia amongst Chinese preschoolers. *International Journal of Environmental Research and Public Health* 17(3): 1056.

The Council on Communications and Media. (2011). Media use by children younger than 2 years. *Pediatrics* 128(5): 1040–1045.

Canadian Paediatric Society, Digital Health Task Force. (2017). Screen time and young children: Promoting health and development in a digital world. *Paediatrics & Child Health* 22(8): 461–468.

Tamana, S.K. et al. (2019). Screen-time is associated with inattention problems in preschoolers: Results from the CHILD birth cohort study. *PLoS ONE* 14(4): e0213995.

Acknowledgements

Writing a book is just like having a baby: you can't do it alone. This book is the result of great support over the past few years. It feels like it has been created after multiple IVF treatments and birthed only through the care of a dedicated team of specialists for whom I am so thankful.

Cindy Webber, thank you for recognising the potential of packaging my content as a book and keeping my hope alive. Lee le Roux, your calm and strategic point of view has been so critical in getting this book out of my head and into print.

To the families I have worked with, the reason I started writing this book, thank you. I have learnt so much from your strength and your stories.

To my mom-tribe, who know all my flaws and all my craziness, thank you for being there since the beginning, whether I was in the trenches or celebrating the wins. Annalis Venter, Jesse Kumm, Alex White, Kate Stuart, Kathryn van Dongen and Robyn von

Ginkel, your collective wisdom and humour have made motherhood that much easier. Thank you for your friendship.

To my husband, Lester, you are a creative genius. I would not have my kids, my practice or any of my corporate identity without you. The incredible images and infographics in this book are thanks to you and those whom you have trained, like Amy Ahrens and Keshia Abrahams. Thank you!

To my sister, Sherinne Winderley, thank you for the title of this book and the many hilarious conversations that have led up to its completion.

To my mother-in-law, Karen Atkinson, thank you for stepping in to look after my kids whenever I needed to get some work done.

And finally, to my mother, Karen Simpson, thank you for being a great mother to me. What a privilege to have you in my corner.

It really does take a village.

Index

G

GA see gestational age (GA)

gastro-oesophageal reflux disease (GORD) 32, 160-161

genes 27-28, 41-42, 146-147, 169

genetics 27, 42, 61, 74, 147, 185

genetics and culture 26, 27, 29

gestational age (GA) 26, 29, 36-37, 40, 42, 95, 185

GORD see gastro-oesophageal reflux disease (GORD)

grommets 165

gross motor 185, 187
  development 40, 223, 233, 245
  skills 191, 222, 244

H

hormones 111, 153
  bonding 47, 50
  love 68
  melatonin 152, 158
  oxytocin 47, 68, 138-139, 142, 153, 168
  prolactin 47, 68, 90
  sleep 158
  stress 47, 68, 115, 168
hypotonic 31

I

intrauterine growth restriction (IUGR) 39

iron 112, 122-123

J

journey 12, 30, 47, 81, 86, 167, 185, 269

K

knowledge 145

kale 118

L

La Leche League International 92, 104, 124, 142

lactation consultant 87-88, 94, 104,126

language 26
  body 198-199
  development 38
  receptive 71
  skills 191
  therapists 188

low-level laser therapy (LLLT) 88

M

mastitis 90-91

maternity leave 12, 51-52, 76

maturational processes 221

medical conditions 220, 227

milestones
  developmental 28, 33, 40, 215
  gross motor 231, 232, 238, 244

mineral supplements iron 122

modern parenting 12, 16, 18

motherhood 46, 153, 176

motor cortex 32, 205

motor homunculus 113, 213

N

O

P